NORTH AMERICAN RAILWAYS

Canadian Pacific diesel
train at London, Ontario.

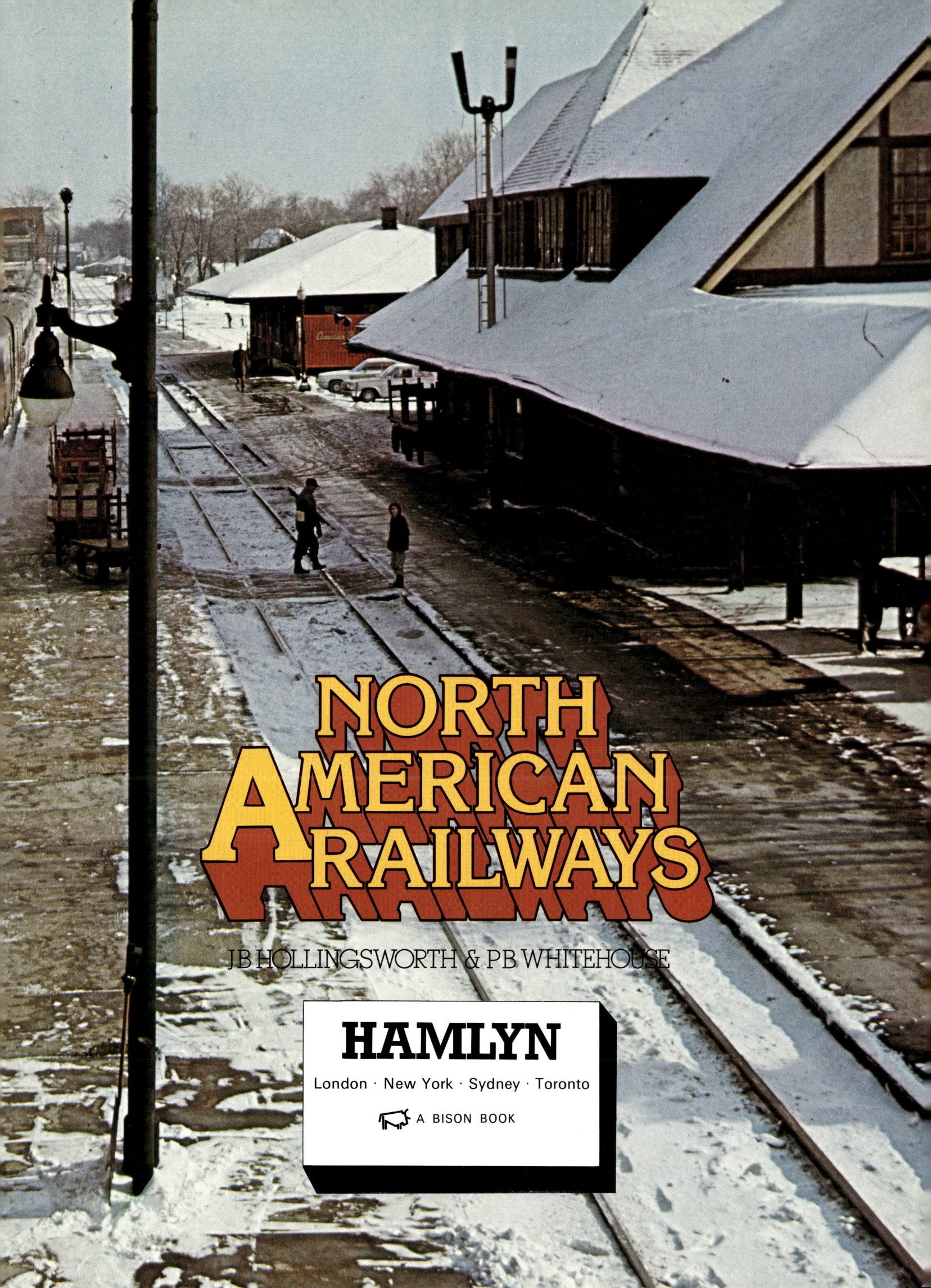

NORTH AMERICAN RAILWAYS

JB HOLLINGSWORTH & PB WHITEHOUSE

HAMLYN

London · New York · Sydney · Toronto

A BISON BOOK

CONTENTS

Published by
The Hamlyn Publishing Group Limited
London · New York · Sydney · Toronto
Astronaut House, Hounslow Road
Feltham, Middlesex

Copyright © 1977 by Bison Books Limited

Produced by
Bison Books Limited
4 Cromwell Place
London SW7

ISBN: 0600 376 443

Printed in Hong Kong
Second impression 1979

The 2-8-4 No 759 from the Nickel Plate Road steaming out on the Railroad Centennial Special.

Flat lying smoke marks the trail of the Railroad Centennial Special.

INTRODUCTION

The story of railroading in North America from its primitive beginnings in the east during the 1830s to the country-wide system that exists today is a romantic and stormy one. From the moment the words 'done, done, done' were flashed across the continent as the last spike of the first coast-to-coast link was driven in at Promontory Point, Utah in 1869, through the years of wars and depression and into the new Space Age, the railroads grew, changed, prospered, faltered and competed in their effort to fulfil the nation's transport needs. The rise and fall of the steam locomotive, the promise and eventual failure of electrification, and the diesel revolution which amazed onlookers by its speed and completeness are all part of the heritage of the North American Railways.

BALT.& OHIO R.R. CO.

BUILDING THE NETWORK

BUILDING THE NETWORK

On 9 August 1829 Horatio Allen of the Delaware and Hudson Canal Company, climbed to the platform of the *Stourbridge Lion* – a steam locomotive which had arrived from England only two months before – and peered apprehensively along the flimsy track used for horse-drawn trains, towards a daunting curve some way ahead.

The year before Allen had been commissioned by the company to buy two locomotives to operate on the sixteen-mile line built to link the Carbondale mines with the coal-carrying canal at Honesdale, Pennsylvania. He ordered two – the *Stourbridge Lion* from Foster, Rastrick & Co of Stourbridge and a more sophisticated machine, the *America*, from Robert Stephenson & Co. Now he was about to back his judgment by becoming the first man in America to drive a working steam locomotive. And, judging from what he wrote fifty years later, he viewed his historic mission with a certain amount of trepidation.

'I took my position on the platform of the locomotive alone', he remembered, 'and with my hand on the throttle valve said: "If there is any danger in this ride it is not necessary that the life and limb of more than one be subjected to danger." The locomotive, having no train behind it, answered at once to the movement of the hand; soon the straight line was run over, and the curve reached and passed before there was time to think.

'Soon I was out of sight in the three miles ride alone in the woods of Pennsylvania. I had never run a locomotive or any other engine before; I have never run one since.'

In the uncertain hands of such an unlikely midwife American railways were born. In fact Allen's misgivings proved to have some foundation for the rumbling monster proved too much for a track built for plodding horses and both the *America* and the

Above : An old American locomotive with cow-catcher.
Left : The Completion of the Pacific Railroad : Central Pacific's 4-4-0 *Reno* and Union Pacific's 4-4-0 No 119 observe the driving of the last spike at Promontory, Utah on 19 May 1869.
Preceding spread : The interior of an American railway car in the 1950s. The pot-bellied stove in the right of the picture was the only means of heating at the time.

Stourbridge Lion finished their working days as stationary engines. Although the Delaware and Hudson Canal Co did go on to make other important contributions as a railway company – particularly with its experiments in new developments in steam – it was left to two others, to begin etching the railroad on the map of America.

The Baltimore and Ohio Railroad and the South Carolina Railroad both played major roles in the early days of steam locomotion. The South Carolina was the first line in America (and the second in the world to England's Liverpool and Manchester line) to rely entirely on steam power. But steam locomotion all began in earnest with the Baltimore and Ohio Railroad.

Baltimore, a city cut off by a range of hills, was not enjoying the benefits which canal-building zeal had brought to many other places. The solution was seen to be a railway, but the promoters in 1829 had yet to be convinced that steam traction should play a part on the line and thus began construction with horse haulage in mind.

Only a short length of track had been laid when Peter Cooper of New York brought his Tom Thumb to Baltimore in an endeavor to convince stockholders that the future of the line lay with steam rather than horse power. His locomotive was little more than an improvised working model, weighing not much more than a ton. It was simply a small donkey engine mounted on a truck, developing just over one horsepower from a vertical boiler and a single cylinder which drove one of the axles through spur wheels. The boiler flues were made from old musket barrels and a belt-driven fan improved the draught.

But the ramshackle affair proved the point Cooper had set out to make and Baltimore businessmen were duly impressed with the potential of steam traction. In a picturesque practical demonstration, Tom Thumb was pitted against its natural rival, the horse. Both set off pulling similar loads side by side

on a double track. However, just as it looked as though the locomotive had won the race, the fan broke down. Still, Cooper's contraption had done its job and by 1835 steam power was in sole command of the Baltimore and Ohio.

In 1831 the company decided to organize a locomotive competition similar to the famous Rainhill Trials held in England eighteen months before when Stephenson's Rocket won the £500 offered by the Liverpool and Manchester Board. The prize held out as an inducement to entries for the Baltimore and Ohio contest was considerably more valuable – $4000 to the winner and $3500 for the runner-up – though the conditions were more stringent.

The engine weight was restricted to 3.5 tons and rather than a series of time trials as at Rainhill, the company stipulated a month of service haulage in traffic. Of the five competitors, all American, the winner was Phineas Davis, a watchmaker, with his York, a vertically boilered four-wheeler. Davis used York as the prototype for the railroad's first fleet of 18 'grasshopper' locomotives, and although the

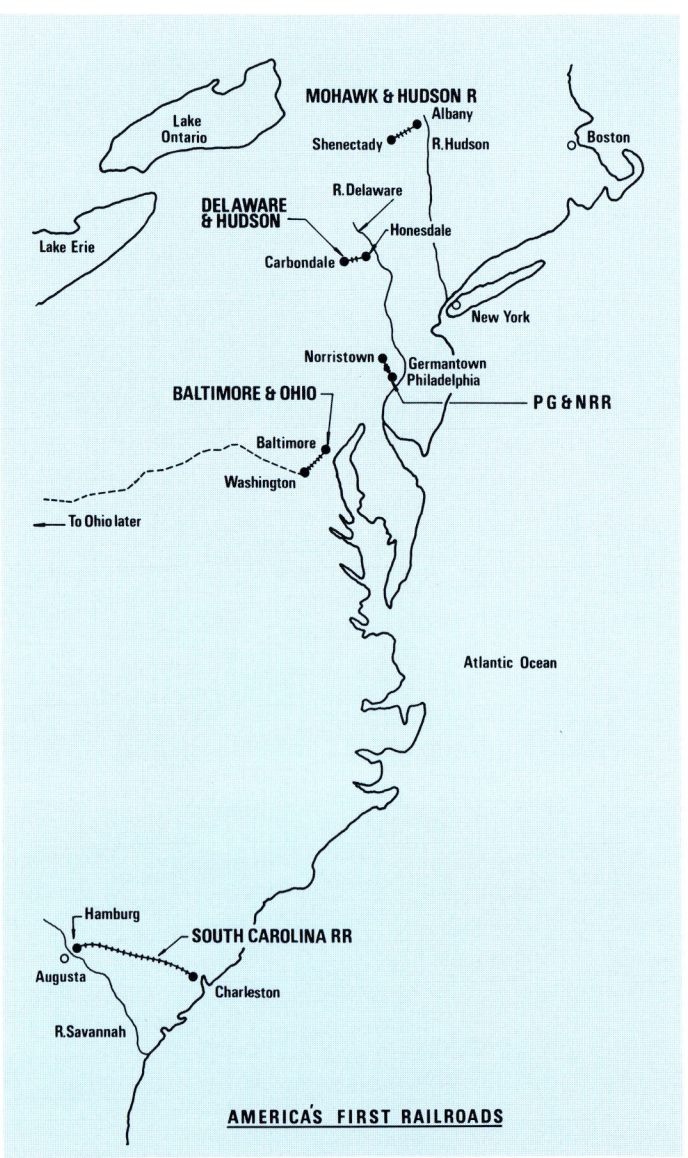

AMERICA'S FIRST RAILROADS

design never evolved beyond its first working pattern, the last of the fleet stayed at work until 1893 to become the oldest working locomotive in the world at the time.

A few months before the Baltimore and Ohio trials, on Christmas Day 1830, the *Best Friend of Charleston* hauled an inaugural train on the first short section of the South Carolina Railroad to make it the first all-steam line in the country. By the time it was completed in 1833, to run from Charleston to Hamburg, it had become the longest railway in the world with 135 miles of track.

The credit for the company's vision in putting their faith entirely in steam must go to the line's engineer, Horatio Allen, who was continuing his campaign in the Southern States. By expounding his simple and irrefutable philosophy that 'In the future there is no reason to expect any material improvements in the breeds of horses, while in my judgment the man is not living who knows what the breed of locomotive is to command', he won over many skeptics.

The legendary *Best Friend of Charleston* had a short but eventful life. Six months after its inaugural run, its fireman fastened down the safety valve. Whether this was, as the story goes, because he was annoyed by the hiss of escaping steam or because he was trying to build pressure, the result was the same. Both the *Best Friend* and its fireman ended their days in a spectacular fashion.

With the success of the first railways, it became apparent that they could play a vital and profitable part in opening up vast tracts of virgin land as well as providing links between navigable waterways and short feeders to existing lines. Such was the zeal with which the idea was accepted that by 1835 established railways in the Eastern States amounted to half the world's total of 1600 miles. Funding was often a peculiar mixture of private capital and State grants.

For example, often the State would grant the company land along the route of a projected line. As the track was laid, the newly opened up land would be sold to settlers to pay for further construction. In order to realize as much money as quickly as possible, lines were pushed forward at a much greater rate than was normal in Britain and Europe where the more perfectionist approach ensured robust construction – and snail's-pace progress.

The American philosophy was quite different: push ahead as quickly and cheaply as possible and make any necessary improvements once the revenue began to flow.

Although this approach held many advantages for a booming country, one unfortunate result of such hasty, independent enterprise (though not one confined to America, by any means) was the lack of any thought paid to standardizing gauges. Though

visionaries were already thinking of a great national network, individual companies were initially only concerned with their particular projects and arbitrary gauges were often chosen, apparently, for no better reason than that it happened to be the first figure the engineer considered.

The South Carolina's five feet, for instance, came to be adopted by the Southern States, while many early lines in the north used a three-foot gauge. The Erie Railroad began building in 1841 with a gauge of six feet.

The advantage of narrow-gauge railways was that they were cheaper to build and equip, though the initial saving tended to be a false economy because shorter hauls and smaller loads meant, in effect, higher running costs. Although subsequent experience has proved the contrary, a broad gauge, it was argued at the time, allowed greater speed; it was also thought to be more expensive to build and maintain. The problem was highlighted when the first transcontinental rail came to be built and a gauge had to be chosen. Many principal eastern lines had by that time adopted what had already come to be known as the 'standard' gauge of four feet, 8.5 inches, while the California legislature had settled on five feet as a State gauge. President Lincoln was known to be in favor of the five-foot measure but the Eastern States wielded more influence. Congress set the final seal of approval on four feet, 8.5 inches as the true standard.

But any contention about gauges was minor compared to the question which had begun as a visionary spark in the early 1830s and had grown to be a burning issue by the middle of the century. Could a railway ever link the Atlantic seaboard with the Pacific coast? The idea of a transcontinental

Far left : The first locomotive for America, the *America,* **was built by Robert Stephenson & Company in 1828.**
Left : A map of America's first railroads as referred **to in the text.**
Below : Pen and ink sketch of the American Locomotive Company's first locomotive, the *Sandusky,* **built in 1837 at Paterson, New Jersey.**

railroad had quickly captured the imagination of pioneering men, but skeptics pointed to deserts, mountains, canyons and Indians, echoing the sentiments of one government official who as late as 1862 sneered: 'A railroad to the Pacific? I wouldn't buy a ticket on it for my grandchildren'.

Though it is difficult to say with any assurance who was the first advocate of a transcontinental railway, one of the earliest must have been Robert Mills of Virginia who published a treatise in 1819 on 'Internal Improvements in Maryland, Virginia and South Carolina', which called for a link between the head of a navigable river in the east with the Pacific 'by a system of steam propelled carriages'. It must be remembered that this suggestion was made six years before the world's first public steam train and 25 years before the opening of the emigrant trail west.

The first *practical* proposal seems to have been put forward in a series of articles published by the New York *Courier & Enquirer* in 1832. The author, Dr Hartwell Carver of Rochester, advocated the building of a railroad from Lake Michigan to Oregon for which, he suggested, the Government should reserve eight million acres of land along the route. Such early visions, though inspired, were doomed to dismissal; at this time the South Carolina RR had not yet reached its awesome length of 135 miles to become the longest railroad in the world.

Until the Oregon trail blazed an overland route west, the only men to have made the perilous journey

Top : Night scene at an American Railway Junction in the middle of the nineteenth century. Above : In addition to the two engines used at Promontory, Union

Pacific prepared two other borrowed locomotives for their traveling display. This was No 119 at Ogden, Utah at the Pacific Railroad Centenary Celebrations in 1969.

were explorers, trappers, traders and missionaries. Among these intrepid pioneers was the Reverend Samuel Parker, a Presbyterian minister, who with Dr Marcus Whitman had established mission stations in Oregon. On his return to the east in 1838 he published his journal in which he wrote with assurance:

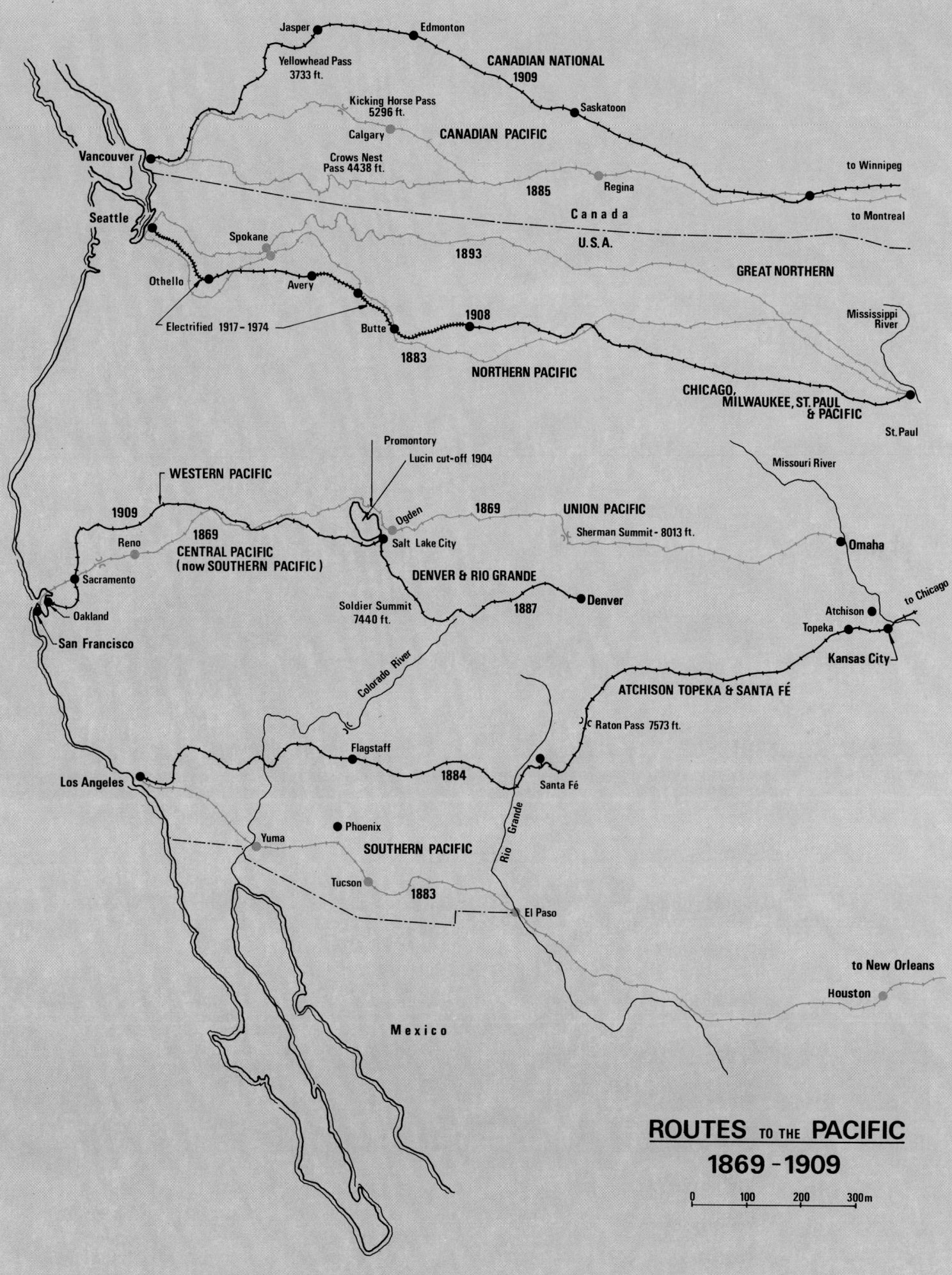

Jasper   Edmonton

CANADIAN NATIONAL
1909

Yellowhead Pass
3733 ft.

Kicking Horse Pass
5296 ft.

Calgary   CANADIAN PACIFIC

Saskatoon

Vancouver

Crows Nest
Pass 4438 ft.

to Winnipeg

1885   Regina

C a n a d a

to Montreal

Seattle   U.S.A.

Spokane   1893   GREAT NORTHERN

Othello

Avery

1908

Mississippi
River

Electrified 1917 – 1974   Butte

1883   NORTHERN PACIFIC

CHICAGO,
MILWAUKEE, ST. PAUL
& PACIFIC

St. Paul

Promontory

Lucin cut-off 1904

WESTERN PACIFIC

Missouri River

1909   Ogden   1869   UNION PACIFIC

1869   Salt Lake City

Reno   CENTRAL PACIFIC
(now SOUTHERN PACIFIC)

Sherman Summit - 8013 ft.

Omaha

Sacramento

DENVER & RIO GRANDE

Oakland

Soldier Summit
7440 ft.

1887   Denver

Atchison   to Chicago

San Francisco

Topeka

Kansas City

ATCHISON TOPEKA & SANTA FÉ

Colorado River

Raton Pass 7573 ft.

Flagstaff

Los Angeles   1884

Santa Fé

Phoenix

Yuma   SOUTHERN PACIFIC

Rio Grande

Tucson   1883

El Paso

to New Orleans

Houston

M e x i c o

ROUTES TO THE **PACIFIC**
1869 - 1909

0   100   200   300m

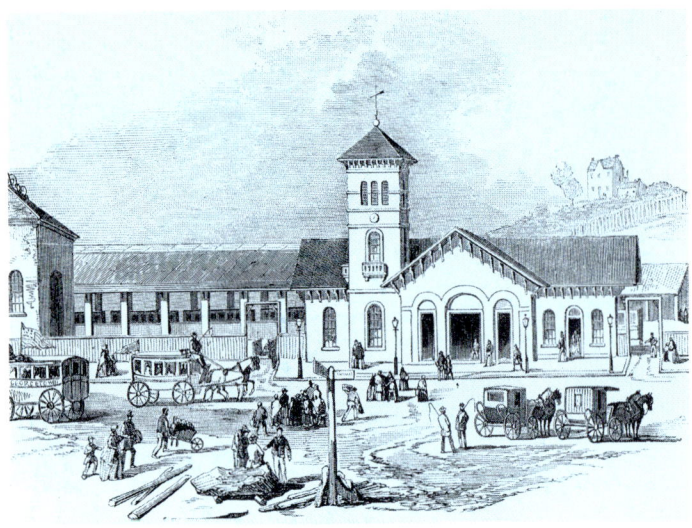

'There would be no difficulty in the way of constructing a railroad from the Atlantic to the Pacific Ocean . . . and the time may not be so far distant when it shall be done.'

These early advocates, though heroic dreamers rather than practical businessmen, did at least awaken public interest in the idea of a Pacific railroad and clear the way for a more feasible plan. By the time one was put forward in 1844, all the implications and possibilities of an east-west rail link were matters of constant public discussion.

It was at this point that Asa Whitney, a New York merchant, arrived home after some years in China. Whitney knew from experience the benefits which could be reaped from east-west trade; he had made a fortune in the Orient and saw a transcontinental railway as the key to a rich trade route across the Pacific. He immediately immersed himself in the idea, putting all his considerable drive and energy – and much of his money – behind the project.

At first he accepted Carver's plan but, quickly realizing it was impractical, formulated one of his own. It was refreshingly simple. He proposed that the Government sell him a strip of land 60 miles wide from Lake Michigan to the Columbia River (amounting to 77,952,000 acres) at 16 cents an acre. In the classic railroad tradition he intended to open up the land with the line, selling off parcels of land to settlers as he went and using the proceeds to push further and further west with no danger of insolvency.

Unlike previous advocates, Whitney armed himself with statistics and a personal knowledge of the terrain, and had an answer for every detractor of the scheme. After four years of energetic campaigning from Maine to Missouri, he had gained the official endorsement of the legislatures of Maine, New Hampshire, Vermont, Rhode Island, New Jersey, Connecticut, New York, Maryland, Ohio, Indiana, Illinois, Michigan, Tennessee, Alabama and Georgia. A notable exception was Missouri which for reasons

of its own, reasons which became all too clear later, condemned the plan.

However, armed with apparently overwhelming public support plus powerful backing from the Senate Committee on Public Lands, Whitney's plan was enshrined in a Bill and brought before Congress in 1848. Whitney was to be the sole owner of the line and receive $4000 a year as manager while the Government would take tolls and regulate its operation.

After days of Senate debate, the plan was tabled on a vote of 27 to 21. The opposition had come mainly from Senator Thomas Hart Benton, Congressman from Missouri, who based his arguments on private ownership. Such power and capital in the hands of one man, maintained Senator Benton, would place 'the blood and treasure of the nation for the sole benefit of Mr Whitney and his assigns'.

The main reason for Benton's implacable opposition, however, became public soon after Whitney's defeat when the Senator himself revealed a plan for a transcontinental railway starting, naturally enough, in St Louis, to be owned and operated by the government. He backed his scheme with the results of an abortive survey conducted the year before by his famous son-in-law, John C Fremont, the 'Pathfinder'. Benton's insistence on keeping the projected railroad on as straight a line as possible west from St Louis – along the 38th parallel – took Fremont across the Sangre de Cristo Range of the Rockies in the middle of winter. There he lost ten of his men and only escaped with his own life after being rescued by friendly Indians.

The fact that he made the journey at all, maintained Fremont, was proof that a railroad line along the route would be viable – though he could offer no accurate data of any use to railroad engineers.

The rapidly growing population of the west – augmented by the ceding of California by Mexico in 1846 and the discovery of gold – changed the idea of a Pacific railroad from a romantic dream to an economic and political imperative. Its viability no longer depended upon the hazy prospect of trans-Pacific trade. There was now a vigorous population of 300,000 in California, mostly of eastern American origin, ready to take advantage of railway communication. There was also the fear that independent government might develop outside the eastern government's sphere of influence.

This anxiety was expressed by Colonel John J Abert, head of the Army's topographical corps, which had already advocated, though not surveyed, a route along the 32nd parallel: 'Unless some easy, cheap and rapid means of communicating with these distant provinces be accomplished, there is danger, great danger, that they will not constitute parts of our Union'.

Both political parties now pledged their support

and three successive Presidents – Pierce, Buchanan and Lincoln – spoke vigorously in support of a transcontinental rail link. In the 1850s, as schemes for transcontinental railroads vied with each other for public and Government support, the railroads of the east, under the land grant system, continued to push further into the hinterland to open up the middle west. By 1852 passenger trains from the east were reaching Chicago.

One positive contribution accruing from Senator Benton's abortive attempt was the general realization that comprehensive surveys, must be commissioned. Benton himself was the first to introduce a resolution proposing a Government-financed survey and the task of surveying the principal routes to the Pacific fell to Secretary of War, Jefferson Davis.

As a Southerner Davis realized he had a delicate political problem on his hands: a southern route would be seen by the Northern majority in Washington as self-interest and a northern route would preclude the South from reaping any of the commercial benefits the line would certainly bring. In the event he sent out surveying parties to straddle the continent along routes running parallel to each other and starting from four separate points, north and south. The northernmost ran between the Great Lakes and Puget Sound; the southernmost, the route naturally favored by Davis, ran across Texas to California.

When the survey teams reported within the ten month deadline stipulated by Congress, the absence of any detailed data once again made evaluation inaccurate and unrealistic. Skepticism was heightened when Davis's final recommendation suggested that the southern trail would be the most suitable. The ensuing controversy resulted in deadlock once

again, but at least the first practical government-backed step had been taken.

The choice of route was finally to come from a young civil engineer, Theodore Dehone Judah, who when commissioned to run a survey for the embryo Sacramento Valley Railroad in California in 1854, revealed himself to be a fervent transcontinental railway advocate. Between sessions of convincing Californian railroad companies and lobbying Congress on their behalf, Judah explored and surveyed passes in the High Sierra.

As soon as he had found a satisfactory route, Judah sought and received the backing of western businessmen who formed a syndicate which eventually molded itself into the Central Pacific Railroad. Unfortunately he died of yellow fever just before the dream to which he had dedicated so many years of his life came true.

The work done by Judah and other dedicated railroaders produced enough detailed and accurate information – unlike previous surveys – to show beyond doubt that the most suitable route was the one that had always been the most obvious: the transcontinental Pacific railroad would follow in the

Top left : Depot of the Baltimore & Washington Railroad at Washington in the early days of rail-roading.
Top right : Union Station, Kingston, New York, a typical depot of the period. New York Central's No 14 from Albany to New York City is at the platform.
Left : The Chicago, Milwaukee & St Paul Railroad's 4-4-0 No 331 was built by Brooks in 1889 but was withdrawn in 1905.

footsteps of the trappers, traders and emigrants – along the Emigrant Trail.

The Pacific Railroad Act was passed by the Senate on 20 June 1862. Two charters were granted: one went to the Central Pacific Railroad to build the line east from Sacramento; the other went to a company called the Union Pacific to build the line west from a suitable terminus in the middle of the continent. Right-of-way through Public Lands was granted, along with free access to construction material. Parcels of land within a ten-mile limit of the track were also awarded.

At this time, however, the Government was concerned with more important matters than the Pacific railway. For a decade slavery had vied with transcontinental plans as the chief topic of public interest. In 1861 it ceased to be a talking point and the American Civil War began. It was the first war in which the strategic value of railways was realized and utilized.

History has often speculated on the outcome of the American Civil War: if the South had seceded ten years earlier in 1851, could the North, without its rail network, have mounted the offensives which eventually broke down Confederate resistance. Fortunately for the *United* States, by 1860 there was a rail network 30,000 miles in length, most of it concentrated in the Northeastern States.

Both sides were slow to realize the military potential of their railways. The Confederates allowed the cut-throat competition between their various lines to continue until the last year of the war when State control finally was imposed in a belated attempt to bring the railway companies fully into the war effort.

The North, however, as soon as it saw the value, pushed forward an intensive program to build railways and at the same time utilized the lines for military purposes. Hospital trains were built, armored trains and even railborne gun batteries were produced. Massive troop movements became commonplace. On one occasion in 1863 a relief column of 23,000 men with horses and artillery traveled 1200 miles in a week to the aid of Rosecrans – an exercise which would have taken three months on foot.

The four years of war cost a million lives and took a further toll in misery and devastation. It also saw the birth of the first transcontinental railroad. In January 1863 Central Pacific ceremonially broke ground at Sacramento; in December 1863 Union Pacific ceremonially broke ground at Omaha.

The euphoria following the jollifications did not last long, however. The Union Pacific's entire resources were exhausted by the Omaha ceremony and the four partners of Central Pacific had paid for their ground-breaking out of their own pockets. The scramble for subscriptions began but it was slow, hard work. Few hard-headed businessmen were attracted by long-term ventures like the transcontinental railroad when quick war profits were so readily available.

The Central Pacific had laid only 18 miles of track by April 1864 and, after a false start which cost $100,000, the Union Pacific reached the eleven mile mark in September 1865. At the eastern end work was further complicated as rail connections east of Omaha did not exist until the beginning of 1867. Supplies had to be shipped up the Missouri or wagoned from Des Moines, Iowa, 133 miles away. Scarcity of labor was another problem until the end of the war when discharged soldiers and freed slaves swelled the ranks of Union Pacific's laborers.

The Army, in fact, donated manpower at all levels. The chief engineer, Greville M Dodge, whose initial surveys, like Judah's, had laid the foundation for the line, had been a General. The consulting engineer had been a Colonel and the head of the track-laying force had been a General.

General Dodge, speaking later of the Union Pacific organization, said 'The work was military in character and one is not surprised to find among the superintendents and others in charge, a liberal sprinkling of military titles. Surveying parties were always accompanied by a detachment of soldiers as protection against Indians. The construction trains were amply supplied with rifles and other arms and it was boasted that a gang of track-layers could be transmuted into a battalion of infantry at any moment. Over half the men had shouldered muskets in many a battle.'

(In actual fact, a large supply of arms was desirable; small parties away from the main camp were constantly in danger from displaced Indians.)

Once the line was commissioned and the construction work systematically organized, track-laying went ahead like a military operation. First an advance guard of surveyors and locators pushed ahead to determine the exact route, followed up by

graders who cut through gorges, graded the roadbed and built bridges. An army of laborers came next and they placed the ties, laid the track and spiked it down. And as each section of track was completed, supply trains pushed forward with fresh 'ammunition'.

In addition to Civil War veterans, the Union Pacific and Central Pacific attracted a motley, cosmopolitan workforce, particularly swaggering Irish in the east and inscrutable but hardworking Chinese in the west. Yet, at the peak of their performance, these strangely mixed crews had become highly disciplined teams able to lay up to five miles of track a day. At the end of the day, with the exception of the Chinese, they were transformed into roistering pleasure seekers bent on indulging in the vices provided by the crowds of camp followers.

By 1869 the two railroads were edging towards each other across the desolate Utah landscape. The grading gangs, in the race for land rights, had already met and passed each other and a Government commission had been sent to arbitrate on the final meeting place. America, about to be truly united by a continental bridge, awaited the portentious moment with a feeling of national awakening.

The meeting point was decreed to be Promontory Point, 1086 miles from the Missouri River and 690 miles from Sacramento. As the two construction gangs neared their goal competition became fierce. With just 14 miles to go, the Central men laid ten miles of track in a day and were the first to reach Promontory on 30 April 1869. With a cutting still to be made, the line from the east was delayed for a week but finally reached to within a few rail lengths of the Central Pacific line on 8 May.

On Monday, 10 May, two trains ground into Promontory and stopped, facing each other at the end of their respective lines: the Central Pacific's *Jupiter* and the Union Pacific's *No 119*. Watched by a crowd estimated at 500,000, a polished laurel commemorative tie was brought from the *Jupiter* and placed in position by the superintendents of construction from the two companies. The last rails were dropped into position and three ceremonial spikes were driven.

Leland Stanford, president of Central Pacific and Thomas C Durant, Union Pacific's vice-president, prepared to drive the final rail spike which had a telegraph wire attached to signal the historic blows around the country. In fact both missed the spike and hit the rail. The two chief engineers finished the job and the telegraph flashed one word, 'Done'.

The next day a scheduled trainload of passengers from Sacramento reached Promontory, disembarked, walked a few feet and boarded a train for Omaha. The line was open.

The first transcontinental railroad was conceived by men of vision; it was built by men with their feet firmly on the ground – and their hands on their pocket books. The high-handed, ruthless, often unscrupulous methods employed by the Central and Union Pacific entrepreneurs were typical of a new race of men on the American business scene. They were often men of courage, immense drive and boundless energy. And they would not hesitate to bribe a Congressman, swindle the public or ruin an old friend in the cause of lining their own pockets. They were the Railroad Barons – the new 'robber' barons.

Yet they were men of their time, a time in which

the only true and honorable business ethic was the pursuit of money at any price – a race after the 'fast buck'. If a railroad emerged at the end, then the means, they would have maintained, must have been justified. The Civil War had produced a glut of profiteers who, though they grew fat while others died, had contributed to victory just the same. Now railroads were ripe for exploitation.

And they were exploited with magnificent panache by men like Jim Fisk who defrauded stockholders in his Erie Railroad of $64 million yet continued to run it; like Commodore Cornelius Vanderbilt who, in a moment of rare altruism refused to buy stock in Union Pacific because 'building a railroad from nowhere to nowhere at public expense is not a legitimate enterprise'. (Since Vanderbilt was in the habit of gaining control of as many lines as he could it might be said that he was more anxious about his own expense than the public's. A more characteristic remark summed up his true sentiments: 'The public interest be damned.')

Arthur T Hadley, a professor of Political Science at Yale, neatly summed up the situation. 'The manager of a large railroad system has . . . two lines of action open to him. He may make money *for* the investors and thereby secure the respect of the community; or he may make money *out* of the investors, and thereby get rich enough to defy public opinion. The former course has the advantage of honesty, the latter of rapidity . . . A Vanderbilt on the New York Central meets a Fisk on the Erie. In spite of his superior power and resources he is virtually beaten in the contest; beaten because he could not afford to go so close to the door of the State's Prison as his rival.'

There were some ingenious get-rich-quick schemes employed by railroad barons, apart from simply cooking the books. Phantom companies would be formed in apparent competition with existing lines; the 'directors' could then sit back and wait to be bought out. These bankrupt lines could be sold at ridiculously low prices to a new company – headed by the same directors.

Investors were not the only victims of railroad barons' business methods; they at least knowingly put their money at risk and could gain limited satisfaction by refusing to put up any more money. The railroad users, the people who contributed directly to the owners' fortunes, had no such remedy. Railroad rates were dictated by the barons, and customers were at their mercy. Often it cost more to send freight to somewhere where there was only one line than to a place twice as far away where competition kept the price down.

At the same time the railroads, acting either individually or in cartels, established discriminatory rates; friends were favored and enemies paid dearly. They could 'make or break' as they chose.

The railroad barons were, as someone said of Central Pacific's Collis Huntingdon, 'scrupulously dishonest'. Yet they built the railroads – and the railroads built America.

Another area in which the public suffered in the interests of bigger profits, was that of safety. While no systems of transport – walking included – can ever be entirely without risk, railroad travel and operations in the 1860s and 1870s were not nearly as safe as they could and should have been. Brakes were inadequate and not fail-safe. Link-and-pin couplers injured and maimed staff by the thousand. Cars which were made of timber splintered to matchwood or went up in flames in accidents that occurred far too frequently.

In 1887 the Interstate Commerce Act was passed to curb the power of the railroads by setting up a regulating body, the Interstate Commerce Commission, to act in the interests of economic trans-

Above : The Chicago, Milwaukee & St Paul Railroad's 4-6-0 No 2000 was built by Brooks Locomotive Works in 1888.

portation and public safety. In the safety field, the ICC played a major role when it enforced such improvements as air brakes and automatic couplers, now universal amongst the hundreds of separately owned and administered railroads in North America. But the ICC's efforts on the other front have tended to bring about results directly opposite to those intended (see Chapter 3).

On 6 January 1893, in a makeshift ceremony, an obscure official of the Great Northern Railroad drove home a plain iron spike to complete the last of the USA's great nineteenth century lines. The event had by now become so commonplace that only the construction crews were there to witness the scene.

The Great Northern was the fifth line to straddle the continent. Jefferson Davis's scorned surveys had not, after all, been in vain. The four later lines followed to a large extent the routes he had outlined. The first to be completed after the Union Pacific-

Central Pacific breakthrough was the Southern Pacific in 1883 which took Davis's recommended route from New Orleans to Los Angeles and on to the Old Central Pacific line which it had taken over in 1885.

The Northern Pacific, which drove its last spike in the same year, ran, like the Great Northern, from the Great Lakes to the northwest coast. The Atchison, Topeka and Santa Fe, from Chicago to Los Angeles, was completed in 1885.

By 1890 construction crews had tunneled through hills, bridged rivers, braved sub-zero temperatures, fought off Indians – and rival gangs – and sometimes died in the attempt, to build a network of 70,000 miles of track – main lines, spurs and feeders – between the west coast and the Mississippi.

WAR
AND
DEPRESSION

WAR AND DEPRESSION

Above : The Interurbans :
The Chicago, North Shore
& Milwaukee RR survived
longer than most with the
aid of *Electroliners* such as
this, seen on test in 1942.
Left : Rapid transit – no
longer were elevated railways built above the
street. Subways such as
this in Chicago were the
norm.
Preceding spread : Boom
years in the 1920s. This
posed publicity shot
which was taken on the
Illinois Central Railroad
at Chicago is more than
indicative of the atmos-
phere of those prosperous
but sooty years.

Looking back, the early years of the twentieth century can be regarded as the golden age of the railroads, when the transportation which they provided was, as never before or since, normal and near-universal for both passenger and freight. Safety standards had greatly improved, the worst excesses of the railroad owners had been curbed and there must have seemed no reason why the service offered should not continue to improve as the two nations prospered. The old lady who on being offered a ride in an early motor car preferred 'to travel by train as nature intended' meant what she said.

On the other hand, it could be said that in general the public by no means appreciated the services offered them by the railroads; in a free society one could understand the dislike of being forced to ship and travel by one mode of transport. Memories of the misdemeanors of the robber barons still lingered.

A watershed in railroad history came as the Pennsylvania Railroad 'the standard railroad of the world' opened (on 15 November 1910) its elegant new station in the center of the city of New York, built at a cost of $100,000,000. At the same time, production of Mr Henry Ford's Model T automobile had begun to make available to ordinary men and women a practical and reliable alternative means of transport.

The year 1910 was one in which to take stock. The Pennsylvania and the Union Pacific lines were spending billions of dollars on improvements, cut-offs, widenings, new yards, depots and roundhouses. Thirty-eight hundred new locomotives were delivered that year (it had been over 6000 in 1905) and the total locomotive fleet stood at 56,000. The route mileage was approaching its peak, close to the 250,000-mile mark; on the other hand, reflecting the work being done and to be done on existing routes, the track mileage of 360,000 miles still had another 100,000 to go to reach its peak in 1928.

Having said that the network of railroads was complete, it should be noted that two new major western routes had only just been finished. Jay Gould's Western Pacific was completed from San Francisco to Ogden in 1909. Gould also controlled the Denver & Rio Grande, Wabash, Western Maryland, and other railroads and was (literally) a few miles short of owning an Ocean to Ocean line. This would have provided a *true* transcontinental railroad, something which had not yet been done in the USA, although it had been achieved twice in Canada.

The other route was the Chicago, St Paul and Milwaukee Railway's extension through the northwest to Seattle, which would shortly become one of the only two major railways to be electrified in North America (see Chapter 7).

A different type of electric railroad enjoyed a brief spurt of popularity during the first quarter of the twentieth century. This was the electric passenger interurban, the so-called 'trolley line'. They flourished in the brief interval between the discovery of electric traction which confined a vehicle to a contact wire and rails and the discovery of internal combustion power, which did not. In 1910 the interurban network was approaching 50,000 miles in extent and still growing; some lines offered luxuries such as parlor, dining and even sleeping cars on their runs. Five years later primitive but more flexible highway buses were in the ascendant and the interurbans were falling by the wayside. By 1925 only a small but distinguished rear guard were left.

On 1 January 1918 the US Government, in the guise of the United States Railroad Administration, took over the railroads in the interests of wartime efficiency, but as so often happens when armchair politicians think they know better, the results were opposite to those intended. The ensuing chaos resulting mainly from directives to re-route traffic by apparently more direct but in fact less appropriate routes, provided a lesson which was well learnt. In World War II the government left the railroads alone

and their performance during that struggle has become a legend. Indeed, it might be thought that the nationalization of American railroads has been postponed for so long because of the failure of this early trial venture. The USA is today, the only country which has not nationalized its railroad system.

One unambiguously satisfactory legacy of the United States Railroad Administration was a complete range of excellent standard steam locomotives. USRA designs were ordered by many lines in the following years although orders for locomotives in general had entered a period of steady decline from an annual production of 2000 steam locomotives in 1920 to 800 in a 'boom' year like 1928; Ford Model T production ended in that same year after fifteen million Tin Lizzies had been turned out. Never again were more than 500 steam locomotives to be delivered to US railroads in any subsequent year. By 1932 the figure was zero.

The number of passengers declined steadily, especially on short hauls, as the Model T and its imitators took hold, and passenger miles fell from 45 billion in 1920 to 30 billion in 1928, but freight volume remained steady at around one million cars loaded each week. The 24 October 1929 was a black day in American history, the end of a boom period that had seemed set to go on forever; at a stroke the railroads found themselves carrying (and being paid for) only half of what they had been carrying in the past. A few went to the wall, but most kept bankruptcy at bay through the lean years which were to follow by desperate efforts of retrenchment and indeed the spare capacity which resulted served the nation well in the war that was to come.

During the war, streamlined lightweight trains – some powered by diesel engines – were developed as a spectacular answer to the new-fangled flying machines, like the Douglas' advanced DC-3 airliner, and were introduced during the modest recovery of the late 1930s. Most passenger trains, still in existence today in North America, have similar equipment. We may note that in 1940 the railroads were still carrying – on a 'passenger mile' basis – twenty times more traffic than the airlines.

Black Monday on the New York stock exchange was followed twelve years later by an even blacker Sunday at Pearl Harbor, Hawaii: on 7 December 1941 the USA and the railroads became totally involved in World War II. By 1944 passenger traffic had trebled and freight more than doubled. New equipment was severely rationed and many skilled railroadmen were drafted abroad to operate railways in theaters of war overseas. Persia, India and later Europe were areas where American practice left a mark which has never been forgotten.

In spite of all these difficulties, the railroads never failed to meet the demands put upon them and once peace had been declared, set off with high hopes and reasonable financial strength to replace their worn out stock. Huge orders were placed for new cars as well as new locomotives, the majority of which were now diesel powered. By the end of the decade, steam locomotive production had virtually finished and the new 'growlers' were coming off the production line at a rate exceeding 2000 per year.

At this time the railroads were as highly regarded by the public as they had ever been and there seemed no reason why the next thirty years should not show the same rate of development as had the last. In 1950 freight traffic was more than double the 1910 figure and, moreover, railroads still carried more traffic than all other modes of transport put together. The route mileage had fallen slightly, to 240,000 miles but while the locomotive fleet was the same in number, the average haulage capacity of each unit had virtually doubled.

Passenger traffic had, as expected, declined considerably with the end of gas rationing and at the same time the shares of other modes of transport had risen to equal the amount carried on the railways, but even so the future seemed promising.

Top left: This typical Interurban electric car belonged to the Sacramento Northern network.
Above: Doughboys waiting for trains at the Pennsylvania Railroad Station in World War I.

Below: Boston & Maine Railroad's 4-6-2 No 3623 hauls an express train. Both the locomotive and the train are typical of what was called 'Standard Railroading'. This period lasted approximately from 1910 to 1950; this picture was, in fact, taken in 1940.

STRUGGLE
IN THE
SPACE AGE

STRUGGLE IN THE SPACE AGE

The quarter-century since 1950 has not been a happy period for the railroads of the USA, but it cannot be said that it was a dull one. In the USA passenger trains now cover only one-tenth of the network and – with a few honorable exceptions – these are only able to run with the help of a substantial subsidy from the taxpayer. The railroads' share of the nation's freight traffic has also slid from 60 percent in 1950 to 37 percent – and still falling – in 1975. Return on investment has been incredibly low.

In the case of passenger trains, the turning point was the coming of jet aircraft in the 1960s; these were so fast compared with their 'propellered' predecessors that adding that extra hour to get to and from the airports at either end of the trip became less important. Furthermore, they were so smooth and comfortable that the roominess of the train ceased to matter. Until this time the railroads had remained in competition with aircraft, buying luxury equipment and wooing the passenger. Pushing passenger trains further downhill at the lower end of the market, were turnpikes and interstate highway improvements which were easing the strain of driving as well as reducing the traveling times of long-distance buses. Rail passenger fares suffered accordingly.

Retrenchment was the order of the day. In some cases amenities disappeared; Southern Pacific's *Sunset Limited*, once a luxury train, between New Orleans and Los Angeles, for example, had no sleepers or diners (only an automat) in spite of the 44-hour journey time. In individual cases passenger service was abandoned with the approval of the Interstate Commerce Commission after exhaustive and lengthy enquiries. In one case, when permission to discontinue service was finally received, an exasperated management did so there and then,

Above : Modernization for steam: Norfolk & Western's Class K-2 4-6-2 No 134 leaves the 'lubritorium' at Williamson depot, circa 1950.
Left : The Amtrak Train 3, the *Southwest Limited*, arrives at Los Angeles' Union Station from Chicago. Included in the train are baggage cars, a single-to-double-decker aerodynamic adaptor coach, double-deck coaches and ordinary coaches including a dome car.
Preceding spread : New York, Ontario & Western Railroad : the OW or 'Old Woman' was, in 1959, the first major railroad to close down abandoning over 500 miles of track.

Above: Public ownership provided the New York subway trains with new air-conditioned stock – in sharp contrast with the old so-called 'Block cars' which were usually open.

Bottom right: The double-headed New York-Chicago Express in the Pennsylvania Railroad's Tuscan red livery rounds the famous horseshoe curve near Altoona, Pa.

leaving a few remaining passengers stranded half-way to their destination.

Two new types of passenger train service, both originating in this period went against this trend. The first was the 'daisy-picking' or 'tourist' operation based on the premise that people might wish to travel by train not to go somewhere but for its own sake. This subject is discussed further in Chapter 11.

The second was a small private enterprise outfit called *Autotrain*. It was formed to exploit an idea that originated on the other side of the Atlantic; this train came complete with dining and sleeping facilities on which the passenger could bring his own car. This was a service that no plane or bus company could offer and it alleviated driver fatigue on the popular Washington-Florida run. Although successful, administrative and bureaucratic problems typical of those that beset the railway industry in general, have so far prevented Autotrain from developing on a nation-wide basis.

After the passenger battle had been lost, the trains were ordered to keep running because the ICC insisted that the railroads continue a passenger service regardless of the fact that the people did not appear to want it very much. Losses seriously affected the industry's financial position, as well as its ability to maintain and renew track and equipment but, after a long period during which the situation was allowed to deteriorate, a governmental organization known as the National Railroad Passenger Corporation was created. This went into business under the name of Amtrak on 1 January 1970.

Railroad companies were given the option of handing over their best passenger equipment to Amtrak in return for permission to discontinue long-distance passenger services. Most did so, notable exceptions being the Denver and Rio Grande Western and the Southern Railway. Amtrak provides passenger service on a few selected routes with the help of a federal subsidy and a few Amtrak routes are subsidized by state or local city authorities. Although Amtrak has some of the faults typical of government organizations, it has now reached a point where it can put new locomotives and cars into service to replace the out-of-date, second-hand ones it inherited. Individual Amtrak trains are described in Chapter 11.

However, Amtrak has created a problem for Autotrain; having exclusive rights to railway

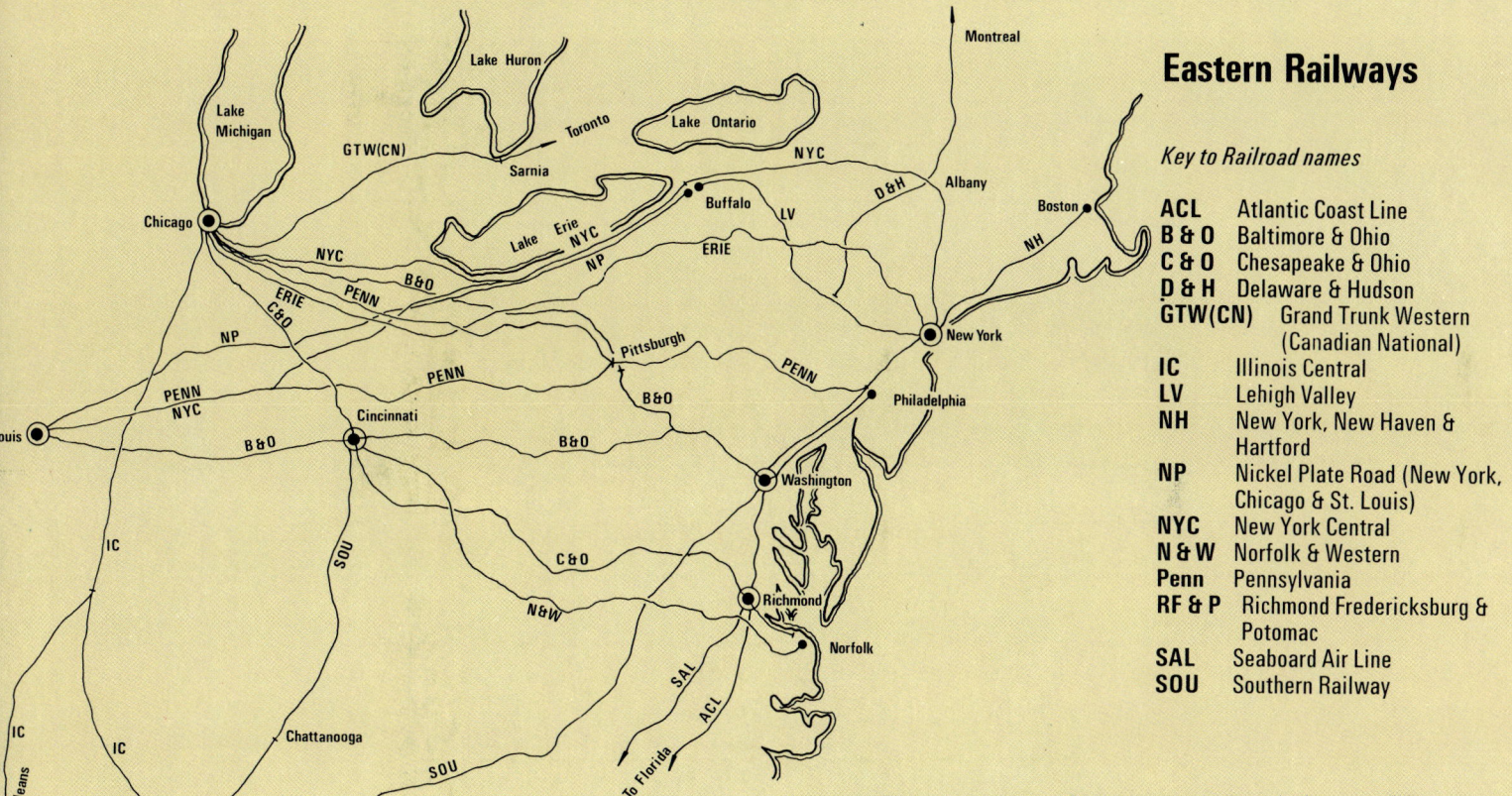

Eastern Railways

Key to Railroad names

ACL   Atlantic Coast Line
B & O   Baltimore & Ohio
C & O   Chesapeake & Ohio
D & H   Delaware & Hudson
GTW(CN)   Grand Trunk Western
           (Canadian National)
IC   Illinois Central
LV   Lehigh Valley
NH   New York, New Haven &
           Hartford
NP   Nickel Plate Road (New York,
           Chicago & St. Louis)
NYC   New York Central
N & W   Norfolk & Western
Penn   Pennsylvania
RF & P   Richmond Fredericksburg &
           Potomac
SAL   Seaboard Air Line
SOU   Southern Railway

passenger transportation Amtrak will not allow Autotrain on its routes. On the other hand, Amtrak cannot run its own 'autotrain' because the owners of the lines on which Amtrak trains run state that Amtrak cannot carry freight, only passengers. These problems will no doubt be resolved, but in the meantime there are only two autotrain services in the USA compared with, for example, 143 in Europe.

The picture now portrays nationalized subsidized long-distance passenger service on a smaller scale than in the past, and offering journeys only on the most important routes, in modest comfort rather than luxury. Of course, people who decide to travel by train nowadays do so (at least over distances of 500 miles or more) for the pleasure of the journey itself and the sight of the passing American scenery.

The '0815 to the city' business is another loss-maker for the railroads, but here the trouble is not competition as much as the refusal of local authorities to allow an economic fare to be charged. The Southern Pacific Railroad, saddled with its Peninsular commuter service south from San Francisco, recently offered to donate free mini-vans to its regular riders if allowed to discontinue its rail service. At present Southern Pacific spends $3 for every $1 it receives in fares.

Elsewhere, particularly in areas where the railroads are not so well-heeled and, perhaps, not so much in control of their own destinies as SP, commuter service is sometimes subsidized by State funds. Other cities and areas run their own local railroads and have done so for many years. Their history runs from New York's subways and Chicago's EL to San Francisco's recent BART system (part subway, part elevated); however, the story of rapid transit, so popular in the otherwise quiet 1960s and 1970s, is a subject on its own and can only be mentioned here in passing.

In considering the gloomy history of freight transport by rail in USA from 1950 to the present day, one must regretfully record that, in spite of its being an ideal form of transportation for a land of such dimensions, the picture is one of steady decline. The factors are numerous. Perhaps the most significant one is that the government agency set up to curb the railroad's monopoly powers, the Interstate Commerce Commission, continues to treat the industry as if it still possessed this monopoly on inland transport. Once competition from other forms

of mechanical transport had radically changed the situation, it was no longer either appropriate or necessary to treat the railroads as vicious monopolies. Indeed, such action is the main cause of their present plight; but, to quote a distinguished transport economist, Dr G W Hilton: 'Let no one say that the ICC is ineffective. Anything that can (in 1970) do five billion dollars worth of damage on a budget of \$29 million is more cost-effective than anything else in US government!' This is his estimate of the damage not to the railroads, but to the national economy, of ICC policies on the regulation of freight rates and the control of railroad administration.

Government can also affect railways in the following manner. When proposals for a merger are put before the ICC, one consideration which carries a lot of weight is whether or not people would lose their jobs if two railroads serving the same locality became one. While one must be sympathetic towards those affected, it is not reasonable for an organi-

zation in a competitive situation to bear a social cost of this kind, while their competitors do not.

This leads to yet another aspect of the situation which again militates against the railroads: competitors use nationalized and nationally provided highways, canals and river navigations and to add insult to injury taxes on railroad rights-of-way are used to provide these facilities. Furthermore, since the competitor's facilities belong to the Government, Government agencies tend to favor them in the regulations they have the power to make.

Another problem is the impact of out-dated work rules – in some States upheld by law – whereby trains without a fire and with automatic brakes are required to carry a fireman and two brakemen in addition to a driver and conductor. The rules governing the distance over which a crew can operate are also more appropriate to the 1870s than the 1970s.

It must, in fairness, be added that some railroad managements have failed to maneuver to the best advantage within these limitations. Often there has been too much emphasis on running trains and too little on giving the service the customer wants.

A bold innovator is the Florida East Coast Line, which, during 1965 when it faced a strike, began operating its trains with two-man crews. The subsequent struggle regrettably involved the use of firearms against moving trains, but in the end the FEC emerged victorious. The resultant improvement in its financial position enabled the railroad to revolutionize its physical plant and stock, whereas before it had doubted its ability to stay in business. The FEC is the only class-one railroad to have challenged successfully the out-dated railroad rules on this issue.

The combined burden of all these problems, passenger losses, ICC regulations, subsidized competition, union featherbedding and (in some cases) inept management, proved too much for the railroads in the northeast. One must mention here that the railroad is a superbly economic instrument when long trains and long runs are concerned; in the wide open spaces out west the Santa Fe and Union Pacific railroads withstand a few handicaps like this. But once the long distance freight hauls are broken down into short local runs, the railway is not so efficient. The northeast suffered from too many short runs.

Bankruptcy followed bankruptcy; the first was the New Haven Railroad in 1961 but the most famous (infamous is perhaps the better word) was the collapse of the Penn Central in 1970. Two great railroads, the Pennsylvania and the New York Central, both household names and both serving similar areas in the northeast, merged in 1968. A saving of \$70 million per year was predicted but their managements found it hard to put aside traditional rivalry and truly implement the merger. Furthermore, the economic tide was unfavorable – rising costs and the ICC's delay in allowing a corresponding rise in fares. Thus PC, which ran three-quarters of the nation's passenger trains in 1970, was losing money at the rate of \$140 million a year. Overall losses were covered by short-term loans, but in the end the banks were no longer prepared to renew them. On 21 June 1970 the railroad was forced to file for bankruptcy, joining the Boston & Maine, the Erie-Lackawanna, the Lehigh Valley, Reading and other railroads. The nation's greatest railroad and biggest conglomerate – worth \$7000 million in terms of assets – was no longer in the hands of its owners.

This situation contained the elements of a vicious circle; no funds meant not only no improvements but also minimum maintenance. In this way the incidence of derailments, failures and slow orders increased, leading to worse service and even less income. Mr Richard Spence, a vice-president of the solvent Southern Pacific, once said 'If PC goes down, we all go down. . . .'

The US Government's answer was the Rail Revitalization and Regulatory Reform Act of 1975, which created a Consolidated Rail Corporation –

Conrail for short – to take over the bankrupt rail-roads. It was not nationalization – the specter of 1918 still hung over that idea – but a 'Quango', that is, a *quasi-non-governmental organization* which would, however, have to be funded by the taxpayer to the tune of $6000 million. Conrail took over 15,000 miles of track, 103,000 employees, 3800 locomotives and 140,000 cars on 1 April 1976. Loss-making commuter lines were no longer to be a weight on the railroad; the quarter of the system which had the least traffic was abandoned or maintained under local subsidy. Amtrak took over its first *tracks* (until then it had only run trains on borrowed tracks), when it acquired the Boston-New York-Washington electrified route, the only predominantly passenger main line in the USA. Funds were also made available to pay off maintenance arrears.

All in all the package was a reasonable one and the man in charge, Richard Spence, late of Southern Pacific has a fair chance, not only of making the idea profitable by the target date of 1979, but also of avoiding the catastrophic prospect of the tottering eastern railroads 'bringing us all down'. If Conrail succeeds, US railroading will succeed if only because the enormous government involvement might obtain treatment for US railroads equal to that received by those other fund-consuming darlings of Washington, the highways and river-barge lines.

Far left: One of the New York subway's refurbished stations at Hoboken.
Left: The Toronto subways run on a 4 ft 10.875 in gauge, the only one of its size in the world.
Below: The driving truck of Pennsylvania Railroad's *Pincer III* multiple-unit electric car.
Bottom: *Pincer III* multiple-unit commuter car.

Inset : Union Pacific Railroad's sign at East Los Angeles Station, December 1976.

Preserved for posterity is this Baltimore & Ohio Railroad's 4-4-0, *William Mason*.

CANADIAN RAILWAYS

A s the railway system in the United States was burgeoning on both coasts and forging ahead towards the culminating achievement of the first transcontinental railroad, another great North American network was developing independently in Canada under first British and then national influence. It was a network which eventually evolved into a unique system in which both publicly and privately owned lines would operate successfully side by side.

The first railway in Canada, the Champlain and St Lawrence, opened in 1836 to provide a portage system between Lake Champlain and the St Lawrence river at Montreal. The line became part of the British-owned Grand Trunk Railway which opened in 1856 to link Toronto and Montreal, thus joining Ontario and Quebec (then Upper and Lower Canada).

The Champlain and St Lawrence adopted a gauge of five feet, six inches which, until standardization was applied, became the official Grand Trunk gauge and was used to a large extent throughout Canada. The Grand Trunk, with branch lines and takeovers, eventually controlled 4800 miles of track from Quebec to Chicago in the US.

Although the building of the Canadian network was a British colonial undertaking, the conditions and incentives for growth were more akin to those in the United States. Apart from vast tracts of land needing to be opened up for settlement, there were strong political considerations; newly settled provinces needed rapid and easy communications with the rest of the scattered Dominion in order to secure their loyalty to the Crown.

This pressing need led to early examples of publicly owned railways in Canada. Using public funds, the seaboard colonies of Nova Scotia and New Brunswick were quickly linked with established territories; it was for overtly political motives that

Above : Turbo-train leaves for Montreal in 1974.
Left : The Canadian National eastbound streamlined 4-8-4 No 6402 leaves Toronto, Ontario.
Preceding spread : The Grand Trunk Railway, incorporated in 1952, was to become a major component of Canadian National Railway. In the latter part of the 19th century it entered an agreement with the Federal Government to complete a coast-to-coast railway and began building the Grand Trunk Pacific Railway from Winnipeg, Manitoba to Prince Rupert, BC which was completed in the spring of 1914. Here is one of its 4-4-0s on construction work near Prince Rupert in 1910.

the Canadian Pacific Railway was incorporated.

The Canadian Pacific is today the private sector of Canada's two railway systems. It came into being, like the Union Pacific in the US, as a transcontinental railway company and now controls nearly half the country's network, including one of Canada's first lines: the St Andrews and Quebec was incorporated by the Legislature of New Brunswick in 1836 to run from St Andrews to Lower Canada and was the oldest charter of the Canadian Pacific.

But it was as the builder of the first Canadian coast-to-coast rail link, a herculean task which transcended any of North America's five other legendary nineteenth-century transcontinentals, that the Canadian Pacific was accorded its first chapter in Canada's history.

The first official proposal for a Pacific rail link was made as early as 1857 when an Imperial Commission, approving the concept, commissioned a survey team to find a route. The explorers spent four years in the Canadian wilderness and returned with disappointingly negative results. The leader reported, 'The knowledge of the country as a whole would never lead me to advocate a line of communication across the continent to the Pacific'.

The barriers which had defeated the surveyors were the seemingly impregnable mountain ranges, the Rockies and the Selkirks. But they did make one important discovery – the existence of the Kicking Horse Pass in the Rockies through which the line would eventually run.

It was another eight years before a second and more successful surveying expedition set off. It was organized by the Surveyor General of British Columbia and, whether more detailed or not, it did at least return with a more hopeful report. The team had found what it considered to be a possible route.

But, like its US counterpart, the first Canadian transcontinental had to wait until government was spurred into action by political necessity. By the beginning of the 1870s, British Columbia was becoming increasingly angry about being cut off from the rest of Canada and the other parts of Canada foresaw the danger of secession, or even bloodless annexation by the US. On 20 July 1871 British Columbia was admitted to the Dominion of Canada with a clause in the terms of her union which, though inserted merely for the benefit of the province, was to help shape the history of the entire country:

'The Government of the Dominion undertakes to secure the commencement simultaneously, within two years from the date of union, of the construction of a railway from the Pacific towards the Rocky Mountains, and from such point as may be selected, East of the Rocky Mountains towards the Pacific, to connect the seaboard of British Columbia with the railway system of Canada, and further, to secure the completion of such a railway within ten years from the date of such union.'

Below: Present day map of Canadian Pacific trunk routes.

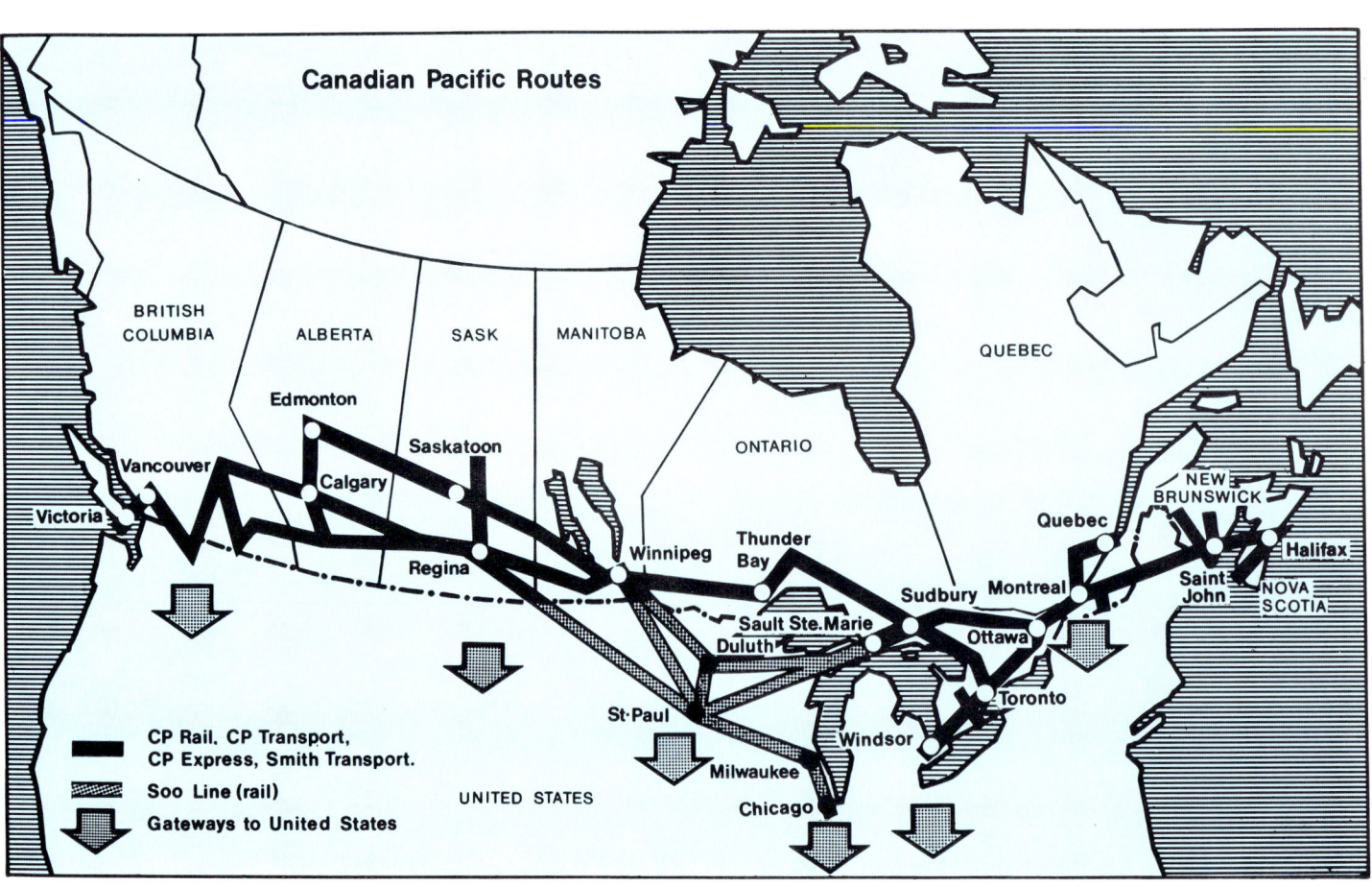

Canadian Pacific Routes

BRITISH COLUMBIA
ALBERTA
SASK
MANITOBA
ONTARIO
QUEBEC
NEW BRUNSWICK
NOVA SCOTIA

Edmonton
Vancouver
Calgary
Saskatoon
Victoria
Regina
Winnipeg
Thunder Bay
Quebec
Halifax
Sudbury
Montreal
Saint John
Sault Ste.Marie
Ottawa
Duluth
Toronto
St·Paul
Windsor
Milwaukee
Chicago

CP Rail, CP Transport, CP Express, Smith Transport.
Soo Line (rail)
Gateways to United States

UNITED STATES

This was the 'birth certificate' of a Canadian Pacific railway – the first official declaration of intent.

Despite this sweeping promise held out in order to lure the province into joining Canada it was another four years of wrangling and contention (which saw the fall of one government) before the first sod of the first Canadian transcontinental railway project was ceremonially turned. The ceremony took place on the left bank of the Kaministiqua River, on the town site of Fort William, on 1 June 1875.

During the period of altercation, in 1872, two companies were formed to build the line: the Canada Pacific Railway Company headed by Sir Hugh Allen in Montreal and the Inter Oceanic Railway Company, incorporating Toronto interests with D L MacPherson at the head.

Under pressure from the Conservative Government of Sir John A Macdonald, the two companies combined to receive a new charter under Allen's chairmanship. The 'Pacific Scandal' arose when it was discovered that Allen had contributed to Conservative Party funds during the 1872 election. The widespread conjecture that the action had influenced the Government on Allen's behalf, allowing him to gain control over his competitor, led to the appointment of a Royal Commission and the resignation of Macdonald and his government.

By the end of 1875 British Columbia had bowed to the inevitable and agreed to a postponement of the final completion of a Pacific railway until 1891. Towards the end of the same year Prime Minister

Above: Driving the last spike (iron) completing the Canadian Pacific transcontinental railway in Eagle Pass, British Columbia, 0922 Pacific time, 7 November 1885.

The hammer is being swung by Sir Donald Smith, a director of Canadian Pacific. Below: 'The Royal Tour in Canada: A Ride on a Cow-Catcher'.

Canadian Pacific Railway's 4-6-2 No 2471 serves as an evening commuter train out of Windsor Station, Montreal in April 1952.
Inset right: The Canadian: an 18-car summer special formation in the Rockies.
Inset left: Canadian National Railway's new VIA color scheme for 1976.

Mackenzie issued a prophetic statement that . . . 'all the power of man and all the money of Europe' could not complete the transcontinental line in ten years. In fact his assessment of the time needed proved remarkably accurate, though somewhat wide of the mark as regards forces and finance.

Sir John's first catastrophic involvement had not weakened his resolve to be in at the start of Canada's transcontinental railway and in 1880, as prime minister once again, he negotiated unofficially with George Stephen, president of the Bank of Montreal, to form a syndicate to re-launch the project. Stephen had already become involved with railways during a visit to Chicago where he had invested in the reorganization of the St Paul and Pacific Railroad.

On 14 September a preliminary agreement was signed in England between the Stephen syndicate and the Canadian Government which led the following year to the British House of Commons passing an Act incorporating the Canadian Pacific Railway Company. The principal terms stated that the company should receive a subsidy of $25 million, 25 million acres of land and two railroads (Port Arthur-Selkirk-Winnipeg-Emerson and Port Moody-Savona which had already been commissioned by the Dominion Government) upon their completion.

Subsequent acquisitions, including the Canada Central Railway, had the effect of bringing the Canadian Pacific's eastern terminus from the eastern end of Lake Nipissing to Ottawa and Brockville.

The colossal task facing the company was even greater than those which previous transcontinental-railroad builders had tackled and surmounted. Legends were born as the track was hewn out of the canyons and high passes of the Rockies. Canada not only had her Rockies but also had miles of muskegs or spruce swamps to be traversed, rocky outcrops to be

Left: Canadian Pacific passenger train 4-6-0 No 626 and staff at old Toronto Union Station, circa 1900.

Below: 'The *George Stephenson* locomotive engine built at Hamilton, Canada West, for the Great Western Railway.'

Left : A modern Canadian Pacific diesel-hauled freight moves out of the yards. The diagonal stripes on the front are to make the train highly visible to anyone on the tracks.
Right : No 6400, seen here at St John, Quebec, on a special working, was one of five streamlined 4-8-4s built for Canadian National Railways in 1936. Driving wheels were six feet five inches in diameter.

blasted, temperatures in the minus forties in winter and mosquitoes and swarming flies in the summer.

Wasteland such as this had to be tamed before the most formidable obstacle of all could even be reached – the north shore of Lake Superior. Here unpredictable waters joined forces with precipitous terrain and near-impossible weather conditions to test the courage and stamina of the construction teams – and the company coffers – to extremes. From government circles to syndicate members, the opposition to the apparently foolhardy undertaking of building across the 'rock wilderness of the north

shore', as it was described, was widespread and solid. One syndicate member, James J Hill, had a particular interest in blocking the north shore project. Hill's plan was to stop the line at Lake Superior and to use steamers to connect the Lake terminus to a railhead on his own line, the St Paul, Minneapolis and Manitoba Railway, which would reconnect with a Canadian Pacific branch on the Manitoba border. Ironically, it was largely due to the forceful and persuasive personality of an American citizen that the transcontinental railroad was eventually built entirely on Canadian soil.

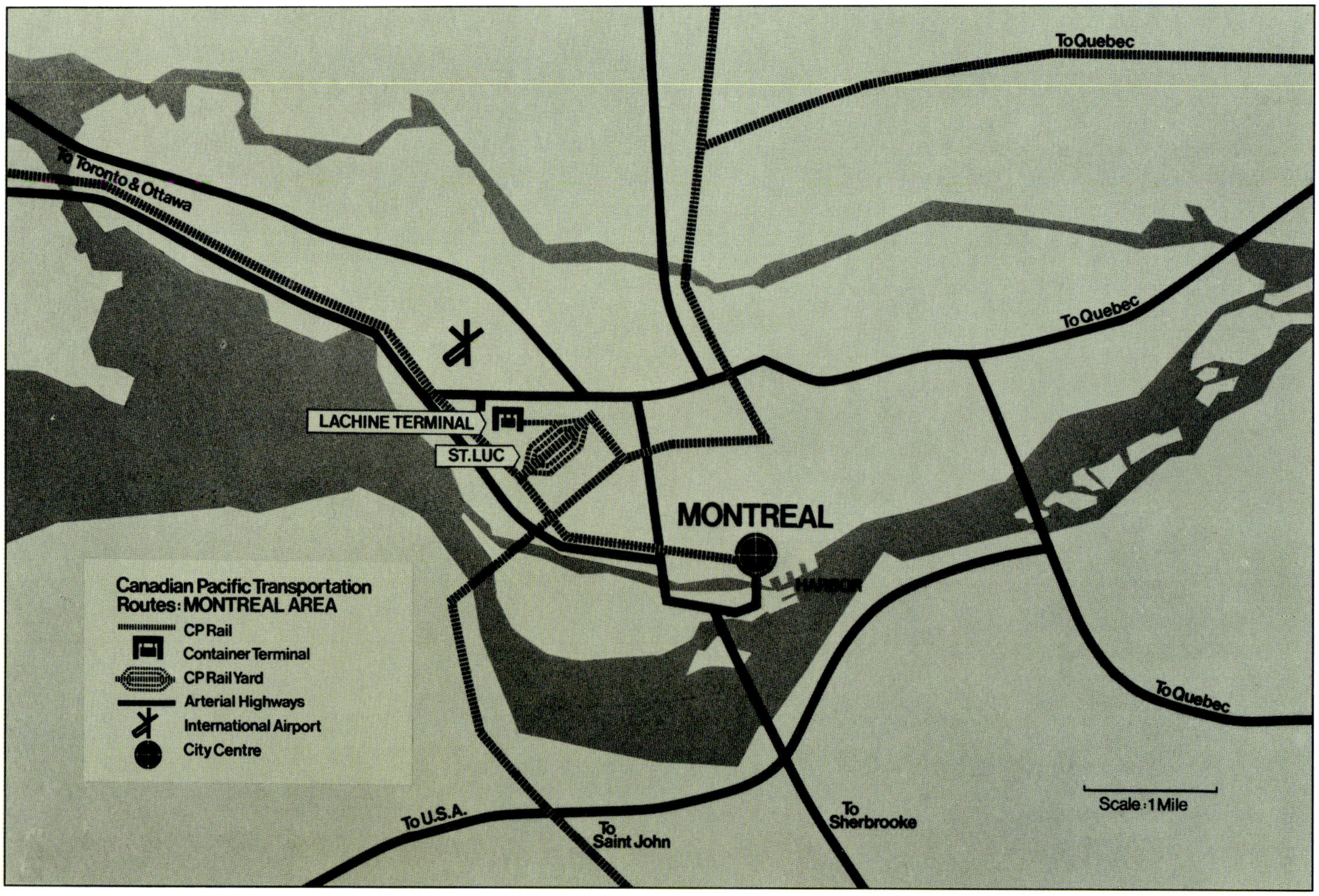

To Quebec

To Toronto & Ottawa

To Quebec

LACHINE TERMINAL
ST. LUC

MONTREAL

HARBOR

To Quebec

Canadian Pacific Transportation Routes: MONTREAL AREA

- CP Rail
- Container Terminal
- CP Rail Yard
- Arterial Highways
- International Airport
- City Centre

To U.S.A.

To Saint John

To Sherbrooke

Scale : 1 Mile

William Cornelius Van Horne, a former Illinois railroad telegrapher was engaged by Canadian Pacific as its general manager at the beginning of 1882. He threw himself into the spirit of the project with as much fervor as any native-born Canadian, and more than many. He was convinced that for the sake of the morale of the new country, the Pacific line had to be wholly Canadian in conception and operation. His implacable opposition to the border plan resulted in Hill's resignation from the board and the general acceptance of the north shore route.

From the Lake, prairie country led west to the Rockies and 500 miles of track-laying across a flat landscape.

Construction across the prairies started in the spring of 1881 and by the end of the summer 480 miles of track had been laid by a work force of 5000 men. Meanwhile on the eastern front, the constant acquisition of existing lines and government contract sections had provided the company with an entry to Montreal, a network in the eastern townships of Quebec, a main line across Maine to the Maritimes and a network around Toronto and in western Ontario. By the spring of 1884 the Rockies had been traversed through the Kicking Horse Pass and work was progressing on the north shore stretch. Van Horne described one stretch as '200 miles of engineering impossibilities'.

Swamps were drained, rivers diverted and lakes lowered. Twelve thousand men dynamited, dug and bridged. One section of track disappeared into a swamp seven times before a crossing was successfully made and at one point three miles of track were needed to achieve a linear advance of half a mile.

An indication of the conditions encountered by the men was given by James Coughlin, a roadmaster on the north shore section, who later wrote: 'We had to ride six or seven miles from the boarding cars to the track-laying machine on open flatcars, when the

Above: Canadian National Railway's 4-6-2 No 5293 in Sherbrooke, Quebec waiting to take the night train back to Montreal on a snowy Saturday night.

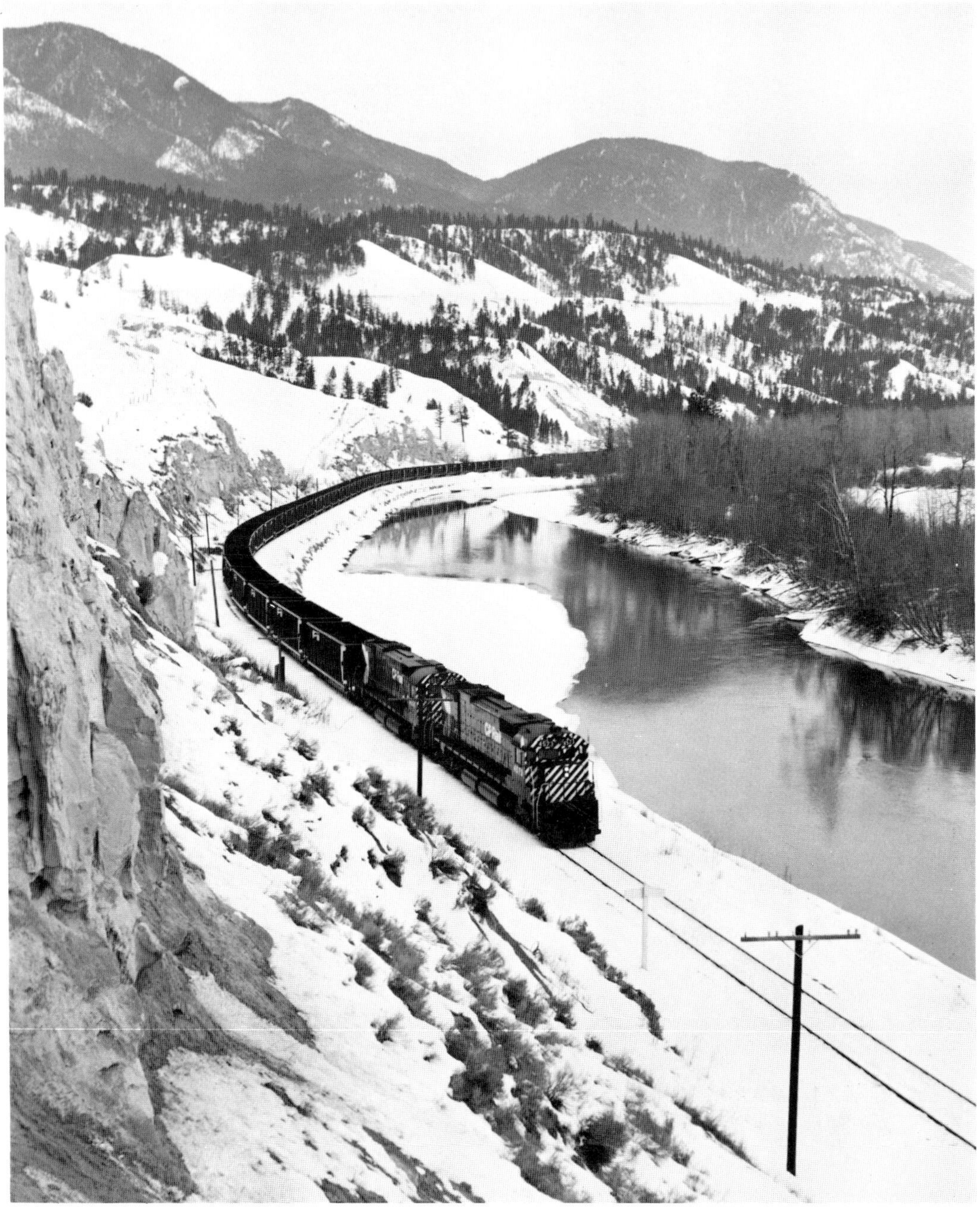

Left: A Canadian Pacific coal train in the Selkirks returns empty to the mines in the very early spring.
Right: In a less glamorous setting than that in which it is usually portrayed, Canadian Pacific's transcontinental express, The Canadian, comes off the Ottawa branch, an operation involving the train crew setting the switches manually.
Far right: The transcontinental express, The Dominion, winding its way through the Rockies in the years between the wars.

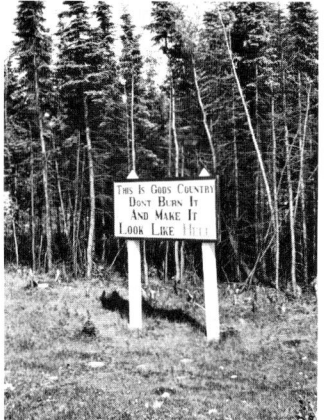

thermometer registered 40° to 50°F below zero. We would stand together in close groups and when the front men could not stand it any longer they would go around to the opposite side of the gang, and thus we kept moving until we reached our work.

'The same method was followed on the return trip in the evening. We had to use a tin stove and a piece of heavy zinc to heat the spikes sufficiently to prevent frozen heads from snapping off when they were being driven into the ties. We often found that the ties would split from end to end, so intense was the cold, if the spike turned on striking the sap.'

But nature was not the only adversity with which the company had to contend. As construction crews were battling against the odds in forbidding terrain, George Stephen and another prominent member of the syndicate, his cousin Sir Donald Smith, were fighting to stave off financial ruin.

Right: Canadian Pacific's freight service diesel with B unit, Jack Fish Tunnel, north shore of Lake Superior, Ontario.
Far right: Newfoundland Railway – the narrow-gauge *Newfie Bullet* (officially the *Caribou*) in diesel days.

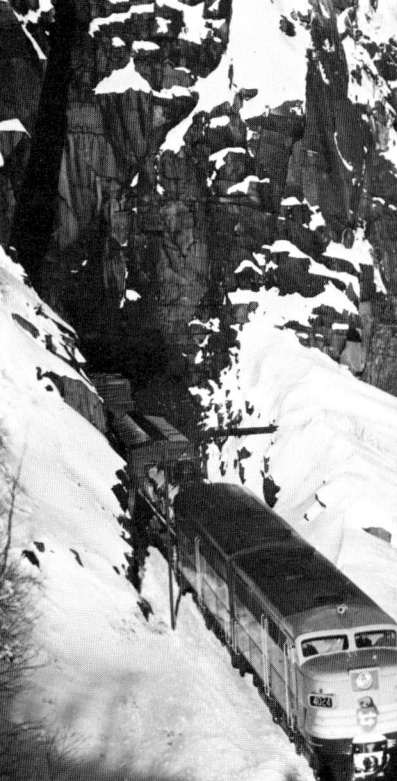

The two men had sunk their considerable personal fortunes into Canadian Pacific. When that was swallowed by the voracious railway, they sold or mortgaged almost everything they possessed and then turned in vain to a reluctant government. When the situation seemed hopeless Stephen with visions of creditors closing in for the kill, told his cousin, steadfast to the last; 'Donald, when they come they must not find us with a dollar'.

Smith, with equal resoluteness, sent a telegram containing one word, 'Craigellachie', referring to the war cry of the Clan Grant in his native Scotland: 'Stand fast Craigellachie'.

Rescue came at the last moment from a most bizarre quarter. In April 1885 news came through that Louis Riel, a half-breed rebel whose uprising had been defeated by General Wolseley fifteen years before, was on the move again at the head of the second northwest rebellion. Seizing the opportunity,

Van Horne put the uncompleted railway at the service of the militia. The offer accepted, a massive troop movement was put into operation through northern Ontario from Ottawa to Winnipeg on the way to meet and crush the rebels. By improvising transport such as sleds and boats between gaps in the line and by completing other sections in record time ahead of the advancing troops, the deployment was made in just four days.

The feat gave Macdonald the opportunity he needed to convince his skeptical government of the necessity of a transcontinental railway for the country's internal security, and temporary financial aid was reluctantly forthcoming. Inside the company, cynicism over the nature of the last-minute rescue prompted a suggestion that a monument should be erected to Riel as the real savior of the Canadian Pacific.

The Canadian Pacific Railway was officially

completed on 7 November 1885 when the last spike of plain iron was driven home in the Gold Range, British Columbia, at a place named Craigellachie in commemoration of Smith's famous rallying telegram. Appropriately, it was Smith who performed the ceremony – Stephen, typically enough, was in England lobbying the Imperial Government on an entirely new project.

Van Horne, by now Vice-President of the company but still a man of action rather than words, summed up the achievement in a fifteen-word speech; 'All I can say is that the work has been well done in every way.' The next day the train carrying Smith, Van Horne and their colleagues arrived at Port Moody to become the first train to cross Canada from sea to sea.

It was not until the summer of the next year that the first regular passenger train, the *Pacific Express*, left Dalhousie Square station in Montreal for Port Moody, and nearly another year, after the line had been extended, that the first train ran into Vancouver from the east. Time had been taken to bring the hastily laid track up to standard, for the need to push ahead as quickly as possible before funds ran out, had meant that much of the track ran over temporary structures which would have to be improved or replaced once the line was complete. Even so much of the construction was still of a temporary nature after regular services had begun. Vast expanses of timber were eventually replaced by steel spans, but some improvements were still being effected well into the twentieth century.

While Canadian Pacific was acquiring a number of established lines to further its transcontinental project, giving an indication of its future role as controller of a vast network of railways all over Canada, the elements of what would become the country's other major system were being formed. Canadian National Railways was officially created in 1922 though the name had been used since 1919. Its creation led to a unique arrangement in which two huge systems, one under state control and one in the private sector, worked successfully side by side often in competition but also often in co-operation.

Though the CNR was never consciously planned as a state-owned national network, it eventually became just that largely through the necessary acquisition of post-CP-transcontinental systems which found themselves in financial difficulties during World War I.

Two factors encouraged the building of rival transcontinentals up to the war – the demand for new immigrant routes and government fears of the results of a Canadian Pacific monopoly. The Canadian Northern Railway, for instance, swept along on the tide of the immigrant boom, grew from a minor network in Manitoba to an 8000 mile coast-to-coast link in less than twenty years. The National Transcontinental Railway, a government project and a part of CGR, was built to open up virgin territory

Above : Canadian Pacific Railway's Budd RDC-276 railcars forming the 0945 hours service from Rigaud to Montreal arrive at Dorval Station at 1048 hours.
Below left : Two CNR 4-8-4s in Brockville, Ontario yard. No 6258 pulled the Queen's train in 1938. Note the special plate on the headlight bracket.

Below : The last great engineering work with which the famous British engineer, Stephenson, was associated was the Victoria tubular bridge over the St Lawrence River at Montreal. Designed in England, the bridge consisted of a single line of tube 6588 feet in length and was completed in 1859 although not officially opened until 1860.

along as deliberately circuitous and long a route as possible. It ran from Winnipeg to New Brunswick through Northern Ontario and Quebec. The Grand Trunk, an old-established network running through Ontario and Quebec and stretching as far west as Chicago in the United States, became transcontinental with the completion of the Grand Trunk Pacific in 1915 which extended the GTR from Winnipeg to Prince Rupert.

The war sounded the death knell for such undertakings, however, as the flood of immigrants dried up with the outbreak of hostilities. The Canadian Northern was the first to pass into state control, being taken over by the CGR in 1918. The Grand Trunk Pacific went into receivership and then into public ownership in 1920, followed two years later by its parent company, the Grand Trunk itself.

At the beginning of 1923 the new publicly owned conglomerate was officially combined into the Canadian National Railways, a generic title which had been used unofficially for four years, to cover not only the latest major acquisitions but also the myriad of minor railways which, in previous decades, had already been drawn under the government umbrella.

Today CN controls 25,000 miles of track and a gigantic freight operation, as well as maintains a declared interest in a continued high standard of passenger service. CP activities, now largely covered by the title CP Rail, rely heavily on freight to provide up to ninety percent of its revenue, though passenger services still operate over much of its 21,000 miles of track. Canadian Pacific's most famous passenger service, of course, is the transcontinental Canadian, the rival to CN's Super Continental, both of which are renowned for their high standard of luxury travel on their coast-to-coast routes from Montreal to Vancouver.

Through force of circumstances a strangely schismatic operation has evolved which, though bizarre by other standards, has proved for Canada to be an emminently successful compromise with nationalization.

THE DEVELOPMENT OF STEAM POWER

THE DEVELOPMENT OF STEAM POWER

Since that summer day in 1829 when *Stourbridge Lion* trundled tentatively along the flimsy track of the Delaware and Hudson Railroad, the idea of steam traction increasingly crept into the dreams of visionaries and gripped the imagination of the public. Now, with its halcyon days past, 'steam' still sums up the unique fascination in which railroads and all their attendant paraphernalia are held. The grandeur and majesty, the legend and romance with which trains and railways have been endowed are all encapsulated in that one word.

Perhaps the combination of juggernaut proportions and mechanical simplicity holds the key to the near reverence which steam locomotives command. For it is the comparatively uncomplicated workings of a steam engine which allow the interested layman a degree of insight into its design, power and performance which would be impossible in more sophisticated machines. This lack of complexity – and resultant theoretical thermal inefficiency – also adds visual impressiveness to a locomotive's already imposing bulk. For it is the blast of the exhaust, the hiss of escaping steam, the clatter of the connecting rods, the rumble of steel wheels on steel rails and the scorching heat from the firebox which are the very essence of railway romance.

Inefficiency in this context, of course, is a relative term. All heat engines must throw away heat in order to work; it is just that the steam locomotive throws away more than most. It must never be forgotten that economically speaking there are many

Left: Northern Pacific Railroad's 4-6-2 No 2448 pulls the eastbound North Coast Limited. Note the Vanderbilt-type cylindrical tender.

Preceding spread: CPR's 4-4-2 Vauclain compound No 209 with duplex piston rods above and below the crosshead and slide bars.

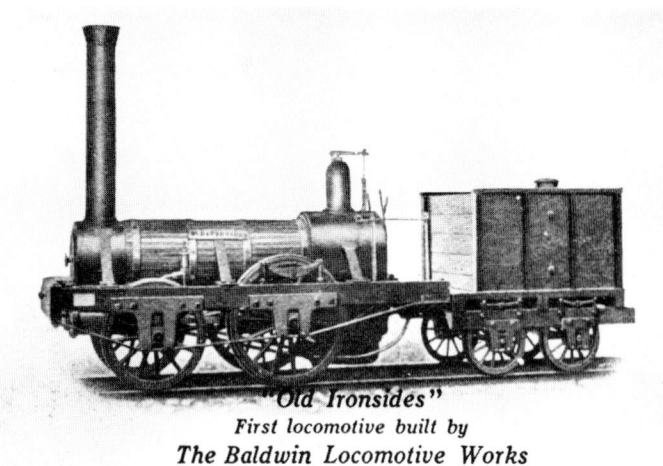

"Old Ironsides"
First locomotive built by
The Baldwin Locomotive Works

other factors to weigh against this apparent drawback: for example, the cost of construction and maintenance, reliability and versatility; in all these areas steam scored high.

The simple criteria for judging an early locomotive were firstly that it worked and secondly that it surpassed its natural rival the horse in speed, pulling power and staying power. Mathias William Baldwin's first engine *Old Ironsides*, for instance, was modeled without compunction on the British four-wheeled Planet class, which only had two rear driving wheels. In fact the ordering company, the Philadelphia, Germantown and Norristown Railroad were so dissatisfied with the results that they knocked the price down by $500 to $3500 and the financial wrangling over the sale almost drove Baldwin from locomotive building. (He did, in fact, continue and his firm eventually produced almost 60,000 steam locomotives.)

Soon Baldwin, like his contemporaries, was devising ways of increasing power to meet the rise

in traffic on the railroads. The first logical step was to increase the number of driving wheels. Henry R Campbell, at one time chief engineer of the Germantown Railroad, was the first to put the idea into practice and early in 1836 he acquired a patent for an eight-wheeled engine with four connected driving wheels and a four-wheeled leading truck.

The work was finished a year later by James Brooke of Philadelphia and the first American 4-4-0 was born. Although the engine, with two driving wheels in front of the firebox and two behind, bore little resemblance to the type which would eventually become as typically American as the Model T Ford, Campbell's locomotive was the forerunner of what, within 20 years, would become the classic passenger and mixed traffic locomotive for the remainder of the nineteenth century. The first of many improvements which eventually transformed the – to modern eyes – ungainly early prototypes into the well-proportioned form so familiar from the 1850s on, was effected the same year by another Philadelphia company, Eastwick & Harrison. They built a locomotive of similar design but with the addition of equalizing beams between the drivers.

The increase in power gained by coupling drivers created yet another problem. Although locomotives of four or six coupled wheels had operated successfully in Britain for some time, the tighter curves inherent in American railroads proved something of an obstacle for rigidly coupled systems. It was Baldwin who came up with the first answer – an invention which led to his famous six-wheel con-

Above left : This locomotive was first used under steam on 23 November 1832. It weighed about 5 tons and had 9.5 in by 18 in cylinders. Below : Note the pile of wood fuel on the tender and spark arresting smoke stack on this 4-4-0.

Left : A survivor of the host of American Standards. Columbia, Newburg & Laurens' 4-4-0 No 2 at Columbia, South Carolina, 1916 – a far cry from its early days as the prime power of a major railroad. Below : Manhattan Elevated Railroad's 0-4-4-T No 189. The driving wheels and cylinders are mounted on a truck which pivots to enable the locomotive to negotiate sharp curves.

nected engine. The four front drivers were contained in an ingenious flexible truck which, by a system of independent side beams which could turn both horizontally and vertically allied to connecting rods on ball-and-socket joints, allowed the front wheels to mold themselves to a curve by moving laterally and independently of each other.

The first locomotive was built on these lines at the end of 1842 for the Georgia Railroad where the performance of the 12 ton engine in hauling record loads soon attracted orders for more of the same design. But, as had happened already and was to happen many times again, complications occurred. Complications and the steam locomotive seemed to co-exist. Excessive maintenance cost prevented this clever design from being in the mainstream of development.

By now many makers were producing eight-wheeled engines on a 4-4-0 plan and by 1850 the constant demand from railroads for greater speed greater power, greater economy, had encouraged experimentation with various wheel arrangements. Baldwin at that time, for instance, was using three types almost exclusively; 12 to 19 ton 4-4-0 for both passengers and normal freight and six and eight coupled engines, weighing from 12 to 27 tons for the heaviest freight. But it was the 4-4-0s which became for many years the standard engine for all but special work.

The first 4-4-0s were little more than enlarged versions of the short-based two-driving-wheel types, but by the mid-1850s the old vertical fireboxes had disappeared and the wheelbase had been extended making the steeply angled outside cylinders unnecessary. The familiar lithe-looking 4-4-0 had arrived to stay for the rest of the century. The first of the new-look engines were built by Thomas Rogers of Paterson, New Jersey, in 1851, and it was not long before 60 percent of all engines operating in North America, both Canada and the US, were modeled along similar lines. By the late 1860s this figure had risen to at least 80 percent.

For certain jobs, of course, the four-coupled locomotive was quite patently out of its class. The spanning of mountain ranges such as the Rockies for instance opened up terrain far beyond its capabilities and eight-coupled ten or twelve wheelers were employed to meet the challenge of the daunting gradients. A J Stevens of the Central Pacific Railroad played a leading role in designing, what were, in comparison with standard designs of the day, gargantuan engines. A 4-8-0 designed by Stevens, built in 1882, and fueled by local timber, coped ably with a rise of 2800 feet in 25 miles on the route up from the Pacific Coast. But Stevens went too far with his *El Gobernador*, a ten-coupled fourteen wheeler (4-10-0) which was the largest engine in the world when it was built in 1883. After a trial in service on the eastern slopes of the Sierra Nevada it was found to be too rigid and heavy for the tracks of the time.

The last quarter of the nineteenth century saw dramatic advances in the design and performance of steam locomotives. Wheel arrangements for general work had largely settled into agreed patterns for specific tasks: the widespread 4-4-0 for mixed traffic; 2-8-0s and 2-6-0s for heavy freight duty. The 4-6-0 was also popular for the heaviest and fastest passenger lines. *Casey Jones*'s immortal Illinois Central No 382 was of this type, not a 'six-eight wheeler' (whatever that is) as the song describes it.

The position, around the turn of the century was that the basic Stephenson layout, which had been imported to the USA with the earliest locomotives, for a steam locomotive driven by two cylinders – the minimum practicable – had been refined and improved but not altered. A boiler with fire tubes connecting a smokebox at the front to a firebox at the rear, was arranged so that steam exhausted up the chimney produced a draught in the firebox. In this way the heat was produced in proportion to the amount of steam being used. No departure in principle from this basic arrangement – and many were tried – ever succeeded in becoming standard practice in any part of the world. Even in 1976, the steam locomotives still in production in China are of the same basic type, the 2-8-2s very much in the American style.

One improvement was adopted. By the laws of physics water boils at a temperature precisely dependent on the pressure; hence, since efficiency is improved by working at a higher temperature, and increasing it leads to problems in making the boiler strong enough, it was thought that further heating the steam after it had left the boiler might improve efficiency. This was done in special tubular elements inside enlarged fire tubes. The idea worked and superheating, as it was called, soon became a universal feature.

It was also noticed that power might be being lost as the steam was only being used once in the cylinders. A second set of cylinders could be provided which would use the steam exhausted from the first ones to produce yet more work. The process was called compounding and had already achieved big savings when applied to steam engines in ships and factories. However, compounding never became standard locomotive practice, although, oddly enough, as noted later, the last main line steam locomotive built for a US railroad was a compound. The reasons were twofold. First, the gain in efficiency achieved by compounding was reduced when, as on a railroad, the demand for power constantly varied;

second, the extra machinery needed frequent maintenance and the cost involved made the process not cost-efficient.

Samuel Vauclain of Baldwins conceived the simplest possible layout with the low-pressure cylinders integral with and parallel to the high-pressure ones and with piston rods fixed to the same crossheads on each side of the locomotive. Numerous Vauclain compounds were sold, but even so, few buyers came back for more.

In this period demands for power were increasing and on many mountain roads double-heading was common and triple- and even quadruple-heading was sometimes necessary. The idea was born of combining two locomotive chassis in one flexible hinged unit provided with a boiler big enough to supply both, so that one crew could handle a train that previously needed two. A Frenchman called Anatole Mallet was responsible for the layout which eventually became universal when the biggest power was required in the USA. Of the two sets of machinery, the rear engine was fixed while the leading one could move sideways on slides as well as pivot, and in this way bigger than normal locomotives could negotiate normal curves. The first example in the USA was an 0-6-6-0 built in 1904; the last was the last mainline locomotive built for any US railroad. Satisfactory road operation awaited the development of the 2-6-6-2, first supplied to the Great Northern Railway in 1906 and what was to be the final type was built in 1909 when some 2-8-8-2s went to Southern Pacific for the Sierra grades in 1909. Six out of every seven were compound.

The drawbacks of compounding did not apply to these articulateds; for one reason, there had to be a second set of cylinders in any case and, their work on coal and ore drags involved, by railway reckoning, an unusually constant power output. So compounding came into its own for this limited application.

Another improvement which was made at this period was to move the mechanism which actuated

60

Above : Grand Trunk Railway's 4-6-2 No 1100, an early Pacific, circa 1900.
Far left: Chicago, Milwaukee & St Paul RR: A view typical of the early days of railroading in North America. Steaming into the picture are American Standard 4-4-0s.
Below left : No 693 of the Chicago & North Western Railway in Chicago station in 1892.
Below : Central Pacific Railroad's 4-4-2 *CP Huntingdon*, the first locomotive to run on the Central Pacific rails. CP later became part of Southern Pacific.

the valves from an inaccessible position between the frames, to a position which placed it outside in full view. Until this time the gear used was – almost universally – the link motion attributed to the English pioneer Robert Stephenson; this did not lend itself too well to external mounting. Thus, another linkage was adopted, which also could give excellent valve timing. This was called Walschaerts, after the Belgian who had invented it 45 years before. The Walschaerts gear (with its close relation, the Baker) was to oscillate the valves of most of the world's locomotives, from this time on in America and after World War I, worldwide.

Early in the new century, the steam locomotive in the USA had reached its final form. The valves themselves had changed from slide-valves (like flat-irons) to the less friction-bound piston type. The need for more power was met by making a wider, deeper firebox, which meant that there was no room for driving wheels underneath it. Hence small carrying wheels on a pony truck at the rear were added to the guiding wheels on a truck at the front. This gave the world a whole new railroad vocabulary, with Atlantics (4-4-2), Pacifics (4-6-2), Prairies (2-6-2) and Mikados (2-8-2) coming off the assembly lines. The names referred to the first orders for these types: the first 4-4-2 went to the Atlantic Coast line for their flyers, while the first 4-6-2 was exported to New Zealand and the first 2-8-2 to Japan. Pacifics and Mikados became respectively the standard passenger and the standard freight power in America for the next 20 years and more.

Below : Pennsylvania Railroad's 4-8-2 'Mountain' type No 6785 exhibited at the Chicago World's Fair in 1933 was the last word in motive power.

The numbers of each type built in the USA

Passenger and Mixed Traffic			**Freight Traffic**			**Articulated**		
Type	*Diagram*	*Numbers*	*Type*	*Diagram*	*Numbers*	*Type*	*Diagram*	*Numbers*
4-4-0	oo00	25,000	2-8-0	o0000	21,700	0-6-6-0	000 000	80
2-6-0	o000	11,000	2-10-0	o00000	700	0-8-8-0	0000 0000	150
4-6-0	oo000	17,000	4-8-0	oo0000	600	2-8-8-0	o0000 0000	200
4-4-2	oo00o	1900	2-8-2	o0000o	9500	2-6-6-2	o000 000o	1300
2-6-2	o000o	1000				2-8-8-2	o0000 0000o	700
4-6-2	oo000o	6800						

High power and a big grate meant more coal and,
indeed, the amount needed in some cases outstripped
the human ability to shovel it into the firebox.
Automatic stoking, usually by means of a screw-feed
mechanism driven by a small steam donkey engine,
became a necessity. Steam jets distributed the coal
around the firebox as it entered. The first application
(using a rather cruder principle) was the Crawford
stoker used by the Pennsylvania Railroad from 1905
onwards.

At this period, just as performance was rapidly
increasing, speed became an obsession with the railroads and new records were constantly being
claimed. By reason of the very approximate timing
methods used, the early ones tend to be regarded
skeptically by modern experts, but there is no doubt
that the speeds were very high and, approximately
if not exactly, those suggested by the times and
distances recorded.

Perhaps the most widely publicized was the
'world record' run of the Pennsylvania Special on a
westward trip from New York to Chicago in June
1905, when an 'E2' class Atlantic was timed at 85
seconds over three miles to give a speed of 127 mph.
The train had lost time due to a hot box on its tender
and it was in the attempt to make it up out from
Crestline with a new locomotive, the 7002, that the

record was allegedly attained on a three-mile stretch
to Elida. The run was recorded by telegraph opera-
tors signaling as the train passed their towers, fixing
the times on the master clock in the train dispatcher's
office in Fort Wayne.

From the acclaim that followed there was no
uncertainty in the public mind that a world speed
record had been smashed but with the wisdom of
hindsight and modern computing techniques, the
7002's 'record' has been dismissed as a little dubious
– as have other famous runs such as the 112.5 mph
attained by the Empire State Express in 1863 and the
115 mph achieved by a Vauclain compound Atlantic
on the Reading RR soon afterwards. But, true or not,
invalidated or substantiated, these undying legends
and the men who made them are integral parts of the
tapestry which make up one of the most romantic
stories in the saga of the railways.

American developments and innovations in steam
locomotion had established the country as a world
leader. With chagrin a British commentator in 1899
wrote: 'Twenty years ago foreign railwaymen in
search of new ideas and improved methods came, as
a matter of course, to England. Today the intelligent
foreigner thinks there is nothing new in English
railway matters to be studied, and he accordingly
betakes himself to America.'

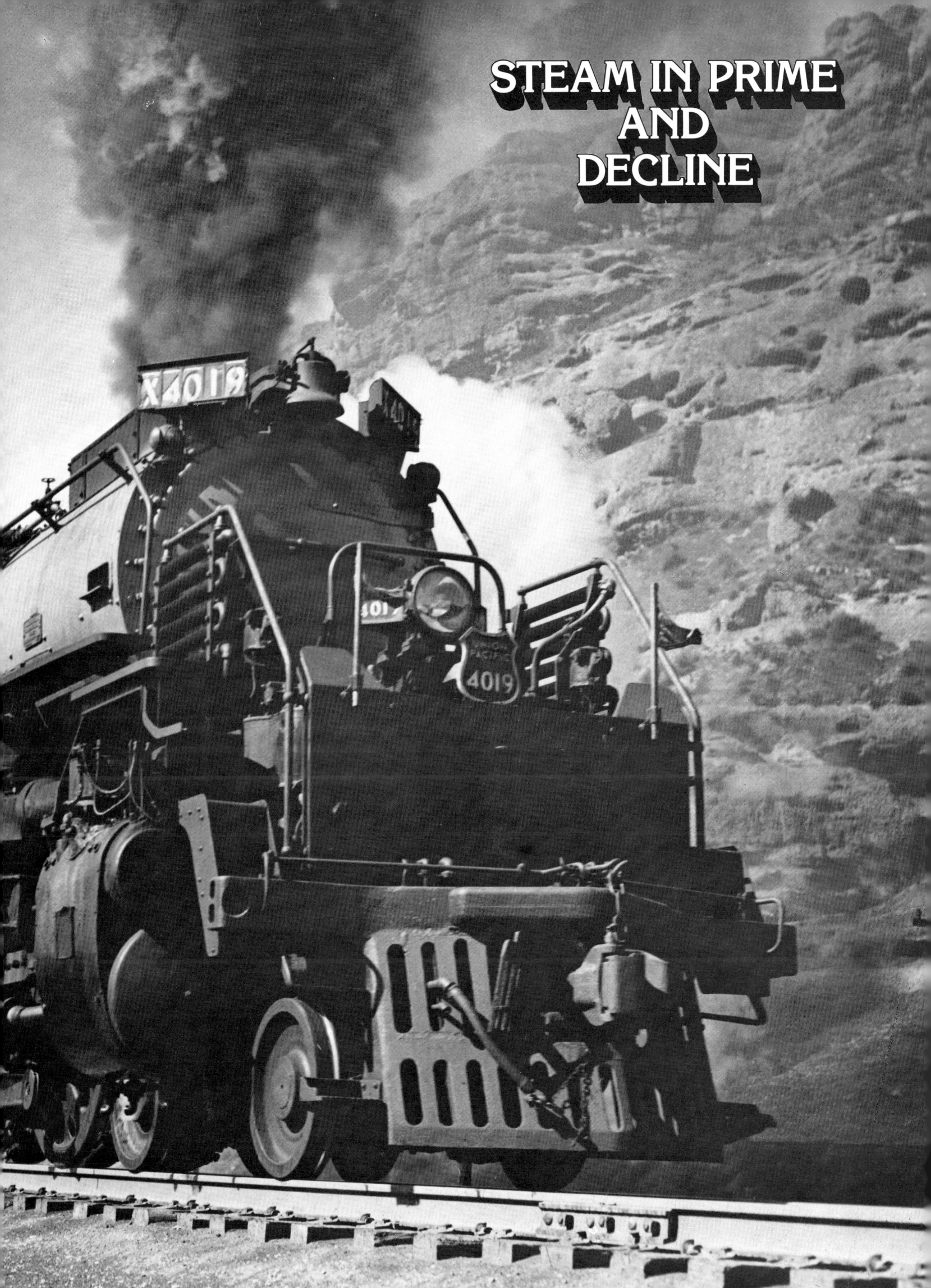

STEAM IN PRIME AND DECLINE

The steam locomotive population of North America reached its peak at the end of World War I, when 72,000 iron horses rode the rails. However, even at this stage of development there were still many details which had to be improved. In fact, during the next 20 years steam was to be greatly stretched and its detail improved. It was 'Steam's finest hour' and David P Morgan, editor of the magazine *Trains*, chose that phrase as the title for his outstanding book.

Improvements and alterations in this period gave us additional driving wheels (up to eight-coupled for passenger service and ten or even 12 for freight), larger fireboxes requiring extra trailing wheels, articulated locomotives which required even more wheels, and so on. The tale of this stretching is best told in the form of a table (page 68).

Left : Chicago, Burlington & Quincy Railroad's 4-8-4 No 5632 serves on the Illini Railroad Club Special, 1964.
Below : A monster of the Rail – six cylinder 2-8-8-8-2 Triple Mallet locomotive *Matt H Shay* of the Erie Railroad. The total weight of the engine plus the tender is 377 tons. Preceding spread : Union Pacific's Big Boy 4-8-8-4 No 4019 climbs up mountain grades in Wyoming.

Left top: One means of getting more pulling power is to add engines together. Here Pennsylvania Railroad has a freight train triple-headed by 2-8-0s
Right top: Canadian National Railway's 4-8-2 No 6069.
Bottom left: This 4-8-4 liveried blue-black with a bright Tuscan and gold stripe was capable of achieving 90 mph.

	Type	Diagram	Name	First built for	Date	Approx. number built
Passenger and Mixed Traffic Power	4-8-2	oo00000o	Mountain	Chesapeake & Ohio	1911	2400
	4-6-4	oo00000o	Hudson	New York Central	1927	500
	4-8-4	oo00000oo	Northern	Northern Pacific	1927	1000
	4-6-6-4	oo00000 00000oo	Challenger	Union Pacific	1936	200
Freight Power	2-10-2	o000000o	Sante Fe	Atchison, Topeka & Santa Fe	1915	2200
	2-10-10-2	o000000 000000o		Virginian	1918	10
	2-10-4	o0000000oo	Texas*	Texas & Pacific	1925	450
	2-8-4	o000000oo	Berkshire	New York Central	1925	750
	4-10-2	oo000000o	Overland	Union Pacific	1926	60
	4-12-2	oo00000000o	Union Pacific	Union Pacific	1926	90
	2-8-8-4	o0000 0000oo		Northern Pacific	1928	200
	2-6-6-4	o000 000oo		Pittsburgh & W. Virginia	1935	65
	2-6-6-6	o000 000ooo		Chesapeake & Ohio	1941	70
	4-8-8-4	oo00000 0000oo	Big Boy	Union Pacific	1941	25

*Selkirk on Canadian Pacific.
(Note: locomotives of an experimental nature, not on the mainline of development, are excluded.)

Perhaps Robert Stephenson of *Rocket* fame would have been less surprised than many might think had he lived to see a Union Pacific 4-8-8-4 Big Boy with 4000 tons on Sherman Hill where, in an hour, 22 tons of coal would be burnt and 12,000 gallons of water consumed. The Big Boys, which arrived in adequate time for World War II, are famous as the greatest locomotives ever built (although some contemporary 2-8-8-4s used by an iron-ore hauling railroad in Minnesota actually take the first place in several respects). A statistical comparison between the *Rocket* and the Big Boy is shown below.

Railway	**Liverpool and Manchester Rly**	**Union Pacific RR**
Builder	Stephenson	Alco
Name	*Rocket*	Big Boy
Type	0-2-2	4-8-8-4
Date of Construction	1829	1941
Cylinders	(2) 8in x 17in	(4) 23·75in x 32in
Boiler, diameter	40in	95in
Boiler, pressure	50lb/sq in	300lb/sq in
Drivers, diameter	48in	68in
Wheelbase	16ft	117ft 7in
Weight, engine	9200lb	762,000lb
Weight, total	12,560lb	1,104,200lb
Tractive effort	1925lb	133,375lb
Fire-grate	5sq ft	150sq ft

Above: A giant American locomotive, this 2-6-6-6 of the Chesapeake & Ohio RR weighed 500 tons. Bottom right: A Chesapeake & Ohio 2-6-6-6 super-power Mallet.

The Chicago, Burlington
& Quincy Railroad's 4-8-4
No 5632 rolls along the
Mississippi River.

Above left : This large passenger Pacific loco-motive 4-6-2 was used by the Erie Railroad in the 1920s and 1930s.
Left : A New York Central 4-6-4 approaches speed near Barnegit, New York in 1939.

This Alpha and Omega of the successful pattern of reciprocating steam locomotives differed not at all in the principles by which they worked; it would be the sameness not the difference which would have made its impression on the designer of *Rocket*.

Other types of locomotive should not escape attention. The Pennsylvania Railroad developed its famous K-4 Pacific which, when introduced in 1911, could sustain a maximum of 2500 horsepower. K-4s continued to be built until 1929 and thereafter to be used until the demise of the steam locomotive in later years; with automatic stoking as well as boiler and cylinder improvements, it could produce 3200 horse-power. One of the 475 built stands today in a little shrine inside Pennsy's (now Conrail's) well-known Horseshoe Curve on the New York – Chicago main line, in honor of its monumental labors on the 'standard railroad of the world'.

New materials and methods made for more mile-age between overhauls. Notable were such hidden things as the use of roller bearings and, most re-markable, the casting of cylinders and other attach-ments integral with frames to make a monobloc solid-state 'locomotive bed'. High tensile steels increased the strength of components and made them lighter.

Speeds at or just above the 100 mph mark became, for the first time (and with steam, the only time), necessary to keep to the designed timetables. The Chicago, Milwaukee, St Paul and Pacific Railroad with its streamlined Hiawatha expresses introduced in 1937 often required such speeds to meet its schedules.

Some remarkable oil-fired 4-4-2s were produced for this service; it was a rebirth of the type after a twenty-year hiatus in its production. Hiawatha

Atlantics were larger than any previous examples of their type and on their 410 mile run from Chicago to St Paul and Minneapolis they were in direct competition with the newly designed diesel Zephyrs on the Burlington runs and improved Pacifics used on the Chicago and North Western's '400' trains.

Apart from their size, the Hiawathas differed from conventional Atlantics in that the two outside cylinders drove the leading pair of driving wheels, while most American Atlantics were driven from the rear pair, and a streamlined shroud gave the engine a sleek appearance far removed from the shape normally associated with the type. Hauling a

matching luxury train, the Hiawatha was able to run at over 100 mph with ease and there were several claims of speeds in excess of 120 mph during trails. The trains were exceedingly popular and accordingly, the load kept on being increased. Nine cars represented the most the Atlantics could manage and therefore, when it became necessary to go above that, some 4-6-4s (the F7s) were ordered, whose ability to 'do the ton' with heavy loads became a legend. However this wheel arrangement will forever be associated with the New York Central, whose tracks along the banks of the Hudson River were for many years the racing ground for its fleet of 275 Hudson locomotives. The other 4-6-4 line was the Canadian Pacific Railway, which underlined their non-USA ownership with a lovely crimson lake livery and Imperial Crown motifs mounted on the valances. A Royal Hudson even now takes tourists on a scenic summer ride out of Vancouver, British Columbia. Apart from being painted in a color other than black, these 4-6-4s were also unique in that they were intended for freight as well as passenger use.

At the same time as the 4-6-4s were in use, the

Top right : New York, New Haven & Hartford Railroad's streamlined 4-6-4 No 1409 pulls standard heavyweight cars near Branford, Connecticut.
Center : The locomotive cab of an old steam engine.
Left : The eternal K-4 : Pennsylvania Railroad tests locomotive 4-6-2 No 5354.

Union Pacific Railroad's
turbine unit No 26 – these
are the sights to see and
the sounds to hear!

2-10-4s (a type called Selkirk in Canada) which were streamlined and also in red livery for passenger service were also being run. Canadian National was remarkable in that it had over 200 4-8-4s (called Confederation in Canada), far more than any other railroad in North America.

The 4-8-4 represented the last word in steam passenger haulage. It took the combination of speed and loading capacity of the 'straight' two cylinder locomotive to the highest limits possible without articulation and the engines were regularly and continuously pushed to those limits. With such size and power at their command, railroads subjected the engines to herculean tasks of strength and endurance. Marathon through-runs were initiated with stops only for fuel, water and crew changes. In the 1940s the New York Central subjected their Niagara 4-8-4s to regular runs of 928 miles with only one stop to take on coal – water was supplied by a pick-up apparatus from track pans. The massive oil-burners of the Atchison, Topeka and Santa Fe covered 1791 miles with six refueling and 16 water stops and 11 changes of crew on the way, while the 'mighty 800s' frequently exceeded 100 mph on Union Pacific's overland route.

Best looking of the 4-8-4s were the orange, black, yellow and silver Daylight locomotives, which were built to haul the Los Angeles to San Francisco trains of that name; introduced in 1935, they completed the runs in timings 30 minutes less than those of the

Top left : CTC controls
the movements of this
Dixie Line 4-8-4 and its
load. Behind the loco-
motive is a CTC tower.
Left center : Southern
Pacific's Daylight 4-8-4
No 4424 is the Morning
Daylight Express at
Mayfield, California.

These locomotives, in
orange and silver were
frequently acclaimed the
most beautiful in the
world.
Below : The Williamson
Locomotive Terminal is
remarkable for its clean-
liness and for its efficiency.

autobiography *Locomotive Panorama* ...

'The depots seemed to be keeping their locomotives only one jump ahead of mechanical break-
down, which when it did occur was of truly Homeric
proportions. In the word of one Master Mechanic
we met, engines would strip their rods both sides and
have their air pumps brought down – but without
even breaking the car windows.'

After describing how impressed he was with the
running of the New York Central RR's Niagaras he
went on to say ...

'At freight engine depots another scene presented
itself. Here the low-duty work horses, underwent a
make-do-and-mend process which kept them running
no doubt, but one wondered at what scale of rough-
riding and failures out on the line ... such activities
went on in poorly lighted dirty surroundings. The
engines themselves were never cleaned and the yard,
the shop floors and even the ambulance room were
covered with a carpet of cinders ...'

present day and with heavier loads. In a land where
steam locomotives other than black were as rare as
snow in the desert (but where brightly colored
diesels were the norm) the brilliantly painted Daylights attracted a great deal of attention.

Many thousands of different designs of steam
locomotive roamed the rails of the continent, and to
describe them all in detail is a task too large for this
book. Examples specified were naturally among
the best but, in the context of the post World War II
situation, they were not typical. One outside
observer, Mr E S Cox, a British locomotive chief who
visited the USA in 1945, wrote the following in his

Such conditions were the product of depression
when improvements could not be afforded, followed
by war when no resources were available. No wonder
diesels became so popular; by 1948 it was not a
question of whether America would go diesel but
rather how soon. The diesel conquest is discussed in
Chapter 7.

The final chapter in the saga of the Iron Horse
was written by Norfolk and Western. The superbly
built and run Norfolk and Western steam power
alone held out against 'dieseldom' for a full decade
longer than any other railroad, entirely on its merits
as the most economic way of fulfilling demands for
haulage.

N & W was initially a coal-hauling line, hauling
coal from inland mines to the tide-water at Norfolk,

Left : Santa Fe's east-
bound Grand Canyon
Limited hauled by 4-8-4
No 3775 overtakes a
freight in the hole at
Cajon Summit, California.
Far left : A Canadian
National Railway's 4-8-4
of the early 1930s is completed at the Montreal
locomotive works and
lifted out of the erecting
shop by the overhead
crane.

Virginia. It was a prosperous, not too big, independent-minded and well-managed company with its headquarters at Roanoke. Management decided that the most economic way to run steam locomotives was the best way to haul freight. First, their locomotives were built to their own specifications in their own shops. Second, they provided their maintenance and servicing crews with the tools for the job and a hospital-like atmosphere in which to 'operate'. Such convenient and well-equipped facilities were almost unknown elsewhere in the steam world. Third, although quite open minded about diesel traction, the diesel demonstration units from General Motors and others which were tried on several occasions and were found efficient, never quite succeeded in making out a case for displacing steam. Norfolk and Western's return on investment on steam was six percent compared, for example, with Pennsylvania's 0.5 percent on electric and diesel.

In charge of the coal drags and mainstay of the N & W fleet were 105 2-8-8-2 compound articulated Mallets, the newest (class Y6b) dating from 1952 and the last big steam locomotives built in America. For its 'hot-shot' freights there were some fine 2-6-6-2 articulateds (the 'A' class) and protecting the Pocahontas express on its runs between Norfolk and Cincinnati were a handful of magnificent 'J' class 4-8-4s. Even the switchers were modern; in fact, little 0-8-0 No 244 was, in 1953, the last locomotive built by N & W and the last steam-powered engine to be made for any US main line railroad.

The indices of performance of these modern steam locomotives' power (such as ton-miles per train-

Left: The powerful Norfolk & Western Railroad's Class A 2-6-6-4 No 1221 steams out of Williamson, West Virginia.
Bottom left: A Class Y6b 2-8-8-2 compound Mallet articulated locomotive of the coal-carrying Norfolk & Western. The 30 engines of this type were the largest and most power- ful ever built for N&W.
Below: Denver & Rio Grande Western Railroad's 2-8-2 No 487 climbing the four percent grade between Chama and Cumbres, New Mexico on the narrow-gauge line which linked Durango with Alamosa.

engine-hour) were, diesels or no diesels, at least as good as any other company on this highly viable road. N & W locomotive depots could service a Mallet in under an hour: this included a complete lubrication job, the emptying of the ashpan and smokebox and the refilling of the tender with 20 tons of coal and 15,000 gallons of water. So often new diesels, serviced in new depots, were compared with run-down steam-powered engines which had been maintained in appalling conditions, but on the N & W the diesels had for once to compete on more even terms; the results indicated that steam could still stay in the game. In the end, however, the problems of being the only major railway continuing to use steam began

Left: The Strasburg Railroad preserved this camel-back 0-4-0 switching locomotive and have it on display.

to tell. Suppliers of components one by one went out of that business, stockholders began to criticize and the price of coal rose – temporarily as it turned out – compared with oil. In 1960 these factors in combination justified the replacement of steam. The deed was done quickly and cleanly; the last fire was dropped when a Y6b 2-6-6-2 came in from a mine run on 4 April. Thus ended an epoch.

However, before the door on steam is irrevocably shut, mention must be made of the 'unusual' and 'odd ball' locomotives which ran on the minor by-ways, and even on some main lines. Oddest of all were the cog-wheel locomotives that worked the USA's two rack-and-pinion railways which scaled the 6288-foot Mount Washington in New Hampshire and the 14,110-foot Pike's Peak in Colorado. The former, all steam, was remarkably successful considering it was the world's first. When Sylvester Marsh the promoter sought a concession from the New Hampshire Legislature, an amendment was proposed to allow him to 'continue on to the moon'. His early four-cylinder 0-2-2-0s are still running and, indeed, a repeat order was executed by the line's own shops in 1972, the first standard-gauge steam locomotive built in the USA for 19 years. The Pike's Peak line, an early victim of 'dieselization', had rather more conventional-looking locomotives from a more conventional builder, Baldwins of Philadelphia. They were Vauclain compounds and drove through rocking levers – which gave additional leverage. In both

types the boilers were inclined forward to make them reasonably level when climbing gradients of 25 percent.

Logging railways abounded in 60° curves, grades up to eight percent and light, roughly laid track. This required locomotives which were able to drive on all wheels with high traction and were flexible about all axes. Three types were actually built and used, the most famous as well as the most peculiar-looking being the Shay, or side-winder. The boiler of a Shay was offset to make room for a vertical steam engine which drove all axles via external shafts, universal joints and bevel gears. All the Shays that remain today in the USA work on 'daisy-picking' pikes.

A second type of logging railroad locomotive was the Hiesler. Its layout is the same as the Ford V8 except that it has a V2 and has eight- (or more) wheel drive. The boiler sits in the arms of the Vee. Some Hieslers also exist today in pleasure service.

The third and least common type is the Climax, where cylinders arranged like those of a conventional steam locomotive drive trucks through reduction gearing, chains and more gearing. No Climax locomotives are known to be active today. They are in fact, mechanically speaking, close relatives of the Mount Washington cog-locomotives.

Eighty years ago, in cities like New York and Chicago, urban rapid transit was provided, regardless of environmental considerations, by steam elevated railways running above the streets. These lines had to be able to turn abruptly at street corners even if the grades and track were way above logging

Top : This Norfolk & Western 0-8-0 switcher No 800 has a saddle tank. Above : A Forney type 0-4-4-T appears on the viaduct above Third Avenue on the New York City Elevated.

standards. One answer was found in the Forney which consisted of a conventional boiler mounted on two trucks, the lead one arranged like the chassis of a conventional 0-4-0 steam locomotive. This marriage of convention, not unexpectedly was completely practical, but the Forney did not survive because the elevated railroads were superseded by subways.

As boilers got bigger, the locomotive engineer remained the same size; it became evident that there might be a better place for him than behind the boiler – hence the Camel-back or Mother Hubbard,

Right : The Pennsylvania
Railroad's turbo-mech-
anical 6-8-6 No 6200 was
the first direct-drive
steam turbine locomotive
built in the USA.
Bottom left : The Central
Railroad of New Jersey
ran this camel-back No
593 on most of its lines.
Far right center : Chicago,
Milwaukee, St Paul &
Pacific Railroad's 4-6-0
No 2219.
Bottom right : Lehigh
Valley Railroad's camel-
back 4-4-2 No 2321. A
camel has been described
as a horse designed by a
committee and this
would seem to apply to
this design of locomotive
as well.

with a cab mounted astride the boiler for the engineer, while an exiguous shelter for the fireboy was provided behind the boiler. It turned out that two men with moderate vision were a better fail-safe proposition than one man with good vision so the Camel-back had to wait for acceptance until the diesel age when it became almost universal under the name of 'hood unit'. Even so, Reading and Central of New Jersey were big steam camel-back users at one time.

Another related development, but one which was applied to some of the biggest steam locomotives in the USA, was Southern Pacific's 'cab-in-front' arrangement. This was only possible because SP

in 1947; the last one, in the early 1950's, was Norfolk & Western's final steam train, the *Jawn Henry*, named after a railroad father-figure, that 'steel-drivin' man'. *Jawn Henry* was a 4-8-0 + 4-8-0 but it failed to keep the diesels at bay as effectively as N & W's conventional steam power. The theoretical advantages of the turbine in eliminating the hammer of reciprocating parts and in using steam more efficiently were never realized on rails although used very successfully in ships and power stations.

The American short-line was an institution; at one time there were hundreds and even now there are scores. These railroad by-ways mustered little in the way of unconventional power. Many used ancient 4-4-0s and 2-6-0s handed down from main line service, others ordered new. Builders like Baldwin and Alco were as willing to accept an order for one light 2-8-0 as they were for 20 mighty 2-8-8-4s and there were others, Porter for example, who specialized in smaller locomotives. Another use for hand-me-downs was switching: the making up of trains and the shuffling of cars. Here again, the most prosperous companies bought purpose-made switchers, usually 0-6-0s or 0-8-0s though some iron-ore hauling railroads went as far as 0-10-2s.

A by-way service for which second-hand power was not usually suitable occurred inside industrial plants. Here can be found 0-4-0s and 0-6-0s, with saddle tanks rather than tenders; it is thought that in this case the present tense is still appropriate,

used oil firing; the 2-8-8-4s concerned ran cab first with the tenders attached at the rear – in this case the smokebox end. Visibility was excellent especially considering the many tunnels on SP's various mountain routes. The cab-in-fronts were an SP trademark; other railroads did not use them.

Another big-locomotive development which never 'made the grade' was the turbine. Six serious attempts at making practical steam turbine locomotives were made in the USA: the first was modeled with electric transmission for the Union Pacific Railroad in 1938; another was designed with mechanical transmission for the Pennsylvania in 1944; and three others along the same lines were planned for Chesapeake & Ohio

although the days when *every* factory had its own steam switchers have vanished. An interesting variation can be found in places where there is a fire risk, but where, also, high pressure steam is available. This is the fireless locomotive, which stores water and steam at high pressure in a heavily insulated storage vessel which looks like a boiler; the mixture stays above boiling point long enough to provide steam for several hours switching work.

As has been related in Chapter 1, in the early days of railways, problems arose over standardizing the different gauges that had been adopted. Hardly had the four feet, 8.5 inch standard been achieved, when pioneers in remote or mountainous parts of America decided that railroads of local interest could be made more cheaply to a narrow gauge. This was at best a dubious proposition: modest savings in construction cost being more than matched by trans-shipment cost when narrow rails met standard.

Three narrow gauges established themselves substantially in North America: a gauge of 3.5 feet

Top left : A typical freight locomotive of one of the smaller companies, Norfolk & Southern, this 2-8-0 was virtually an off-the-shelf design.
Center left : Consolidation : Originally used to haul freight, this Chesapeake & Ohio Railroad 2-8-0 No 1016 was adapted in later years to switching.
Bottom left : Canadian Pacific Railway's 2-8-0 No 3607 switches at Toronto.
Above : Norfolk & Western Railroad's Class J 4-8-4 No 604 is being lubricated.

Below: The sugar hauling Kahului Railroad on the Island of Maui in Hawaii.
Bottom: Newfoundland Railway's three-foot six-inch gauge mixed train follows the 4-6-2 No 196. This was the only system of any size on this gauge in North America.

in Newfoundland; a gauge of three feet almost everywhere from Alaska to North Carolina but principally in the mountains of Colorado; and a gauge of two feet was used in Maine for a number of little railways.

Only in Newfoundland and Alaska are normal commercial operations still conducted on the narrow gauge. However, in the majority of States and provinces of North America the old narrow gaugers are still preserved and new ones constructed in the pursuit of pleasure. But the Newfie Bullet (the official name was Caribou) no longer runs the 547 miles from Port-aux-Basques to St John's behind handsome Baldwin Pacifics or Alco 2-8-2s; the Newfoundland Railway, now part of Canadian National, has been fully 'dieselized' and freight-only for a number of years. Of course, with such a 'wide' narrow gauge (if that is the term) the locomotives differ little from standard-gauge ones.

With the three-foot gauge, however, design differences begin to appear. Early locomotives were fairly conventional little 2-8-0s, of which a few survive in museums and amusement parks. In due course, bigger machines were required for the fearsome

Above : Canadian National
Railway's narrow-gauge
2-8-2 No 1005 pulls a train
of cars carrying pulpwood
in Newfoundland.
Left : White Pass & Yukon
Railroad's 2-8-2 No 72 and
its GEC diesel successor
pull trains on a narrow-
gauge track at Skagway,
Alaska.

Right: Denver & Rio Grande Western Railroad's narrow-gauge train leaves Durango, Colorado pulled by K-27 Mudhen 2-8-2 No 463.
Bottom: Norfolk & Western Railroad's Class A 2-6-6-4 in the Lubritorium at Williamson, Virginia.
Far right top: The interior of the clinically clean lubritorium at Williamson, West Virginia – the locomotive's rest room.

grades typical of narrow-gauge lines; in order to improve stability, the idea of putting the frames outside the wheels was tried, the connecting rods driving on separate outside cranks. This is the 'mark' of the majority of narrow-gauge engines.

On the Denver & Rio Grande Railroad (now Denver & Rio Grande Western), the most important narrow-gauge road in the USA, four classes of outside-frame Mikados followed one another over the years. First in 1906 came the K-27 class, whose squat appearance got them the name of Mudhens. Next came the little K-28s specially ordered for passenger service in 1923. Their name, Sports Model, was based on their low slung, racy appearance rather than a 35 mph maximum speed. Three survive in the D & RGW's own service.

Still more power was needed in 1925 and the result was the K-36. The adjective 'little' would hardly be appropriate as the 36 indicated 36,000 lbs tractive effort according to the railroad's classification scheme and the letter K indicated the 2-8-2 wheel arrangement. Lastly, 1927 brought the K-37s which were interesting conversions of some surplus and quite large standard-gauge 2-8-0s. Boilers, cylinders, cabs, tender bodies and of course, all accessories, were re-used. It should be noted that the cylinder assembly, designed for an inside frame standard-gauge locomotive was also correct (in respect of cylinder center distance) for the outside cranks of a narrow-gauge machine. Specimens of all four classes of 'Mike' survive.

Right : In New Mexico an engineer oils the Denver & Rio Grande Western K-36 2-8-2 No 488 which will soon climb the four percent grade toward Cumbres Pass.

Right center : 'The Pusher on the Monarch Train' : a 2-8-2 No 480 on the Denver & Rio Grande Western Railway's three-foot gauge branch to Monarch, Colorado.

Large narrow-gauge locomotives without trailing trucks led to difficulties because with, say, a 4-6-0 the firebox end of the boiler had to go between the wheels. This meant an extremely restricted fire-grate. The famous little 4-6-0s which worked Southern Pacific's three-foot gauge Owens Valley Branch were helped in this regard as they were oil-burners, but those on the charmingly named East Tennessee & Western North Carolina ('Tweetsie' for short) were not.

The 24-inch gauge is, in a way, the only true narrow-gauge because this was the size (almost) of that patriarch of all narrow-gauge railways, the Festiniog Railway of Wales. It was here that a man called James Spooner in 1864 converted a horse-and-gravity-operated mineral tramway to a steam common-carrier railroad of, since he was an early metric system enthusiast also, 23.675 inches or 60 centimeters gauge. The original Festiniog locomotive *Prince* (still in service on the FR) weighed only 6 tons, but locomotives up to 40 tons roamed the State of Maine on two-foot gauge lines in the 1920s. An appropriately numbered 2-6-2, No 24, originally had a tender eight feet, four inches wide (on a 24-inch gauge!) due, it is credibly stated in Linwood Moody's

Above: Southern Pacific Railroad's narrow-gauge 4-6-0 No 9 on the Keeler-Laws branch. Death Valley is not far away.
Right: Southern Pacific Railroad's narrow-gauge off-burning 4-6-0 No 9 alongside the water tower at Owenyo, California in 1954 on the Keeler-Laws branch.

amusing account of the line called 'The Maine Two-Footers', to a carelessly written 84 inches in the railroad's order to Baldwins. Eventually No 24 teetered off the line – on a trestle of course – after which repairs included a reduction in the width of the tender. Some of the smaller locomotives from these lines in Maine survive on the Edaville pleasure railroad.

Perhaps readers have noted how careful this writer has been to qualify any statement about the last steam locomotives built, by adding the phrase 'main line'. The reason is that narrow-gauge locomotives intended for pleasure use are still in production. And, of course model steam locomotives are being built in various gauges from 7.5 inches to 1.25 inches in ever-increasing numbers for home workshops throughout North America. One such firm is Crown Metal Productions of Wyana, Pennsylvania, who offer their standard rugged simple 1860s style steam 4-4-0s in three sizes – for 15-inch, 24-inch and 36-inch gauges – under the trade name *Little Toot*. Many can be found amusing children of all ages in amusement parks and zoos. Similarly Sandley of Wisconsin Dells offers custom-built steam locomotives for similar purposes.

So, like the sailing ship, the steam locomotive leaves its place in the commercial world for one in entertainment and, in this, its future seems secure.

Top center : Rio Grande Southern's No 20 a veteran 4-6-0 helps No 74 to pull this heavy freight out of Durango in 1949. No 20 is the original *Emma Sweeney* of motion picture fame having appeared in such films as *Ticket to Tomahawk*.

Top right : The narrow-gauge ten-wheeler 'Tweetsie' (East Tennessee & Western North Carolina) 4-6-0 No 8 leaves Johnson City, Tennessee. Note RPO Baggage Coach combine with brakesman riding the tops.

ELECTRIFICATION, TURBINES AND DIESELS

ELECTRIFICATION, TURBINES AND DIESELS

It is faintly ironical that a method of traction that was evolved and perfected by some of the most illustrious names in the field of science – both European and American – to a point where it was being used successfully by major railroads more than 80 years ago, should have come to so little. That has been the fate of electric traction in North America – the home of the first electrified main line in the world. It is even more remarkable that the proportion of electrified mileage to total route mileage is the lowest of that in almost any other industrialized country.

Yet America was one of the first countries seriously to consider the potential of electric traction and to put its ideas into practice. As early as 1837 electric propulsion was demonstrated by Thomas Davenport of Vermont when he managed to move a small vehicle along a short track. By 1850 the government had become interested in the possibilities of electric traction having witnessed experiments abroad, though nothing of any efficiency had yet evolved. Professor Charles G Page was approached by Congress and asked to build an electric locomotive but, when they saw the result, their interest faded. The electric motor had yet to reach the state of refinement necessary for efficient propulsion and Page's rather clumsy attempt at simple electro-magnetic power was not impressive enough to secure further funds.

It was almost 30 years before the first practical developments of Faraday's principles of electro-magnetic induction were successfully demonstrated. At the Berlin exhibition of 1879 an electric locomotive by Siemens & Halske hauled carriages along a track with an electrified central rail. But America could not fail to be far behind Europe; the great Edison had become absorbed with the possibilities of electric traction and it was just a year later that he demonstrated a locomotive capable of reaching speeds of up to 40 mph.

Left: A line-up of the 139 superb GG1 electric locomotives which were built for the Pennsylvania Railroad. Preceding spread: Chicago, Milwaukee & St Paul's 'Little Joe' electric locomotive was originally built for Russia.

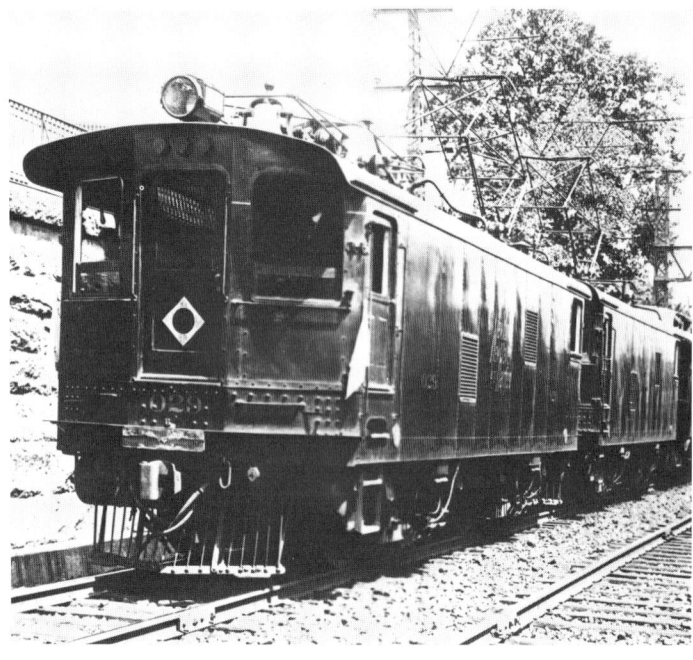

Other models quickly followed but it was the pioneering work of another engineer, Leo Daft, which provided the first electric locomotives which could be put into operation. His appropriately named *Faraday*, *Morse*, and *Ohm* were put to work on the Baltimore horse tramways and his *Benjamin Franklin* saw service on the New York Elevated.

It was about 1895 that another American development, multiple uniting, appeared in an early form. This system was destined to play a major role in the eventual diesel revolution. Frank J Sprague invented a system which allowed a train of several powered vehicles – locomotives or coaches – to be assembled, each linked to a master control in the driving cab, which then controlled all the powered vehicles in the train.

The system, which permitted the now familiar practice of coupling powered units to form longer and more powerful trains, operated on the Chicago elevated railways from 1887 onwards. It swept through the USA and other countries and soon there were 50,000-plus miles of electric railways. London's underground was electrified by an American and to this day the rapid transit lines there call their lines 'Westbound' and 'Eastbound' – or 'Northbound' and 'Southbound' – as the case may be, instead of the more customary (in Britain) 'Up and Down'.

When it came to electrifying the main line railways, progress was, however, rather slow. It was confined to short, problem lengths of railway such as a very steeply graded stretch of line with a tunnel or where a city ordinance forbade the use of steam locomotives within its limits. Of the former, the first was pioneered by steam railroad pioneer Baltimore & Ohio, who in 1895 put the first main line electric locomotive to operate in the USA into service on its new line into Baltimore. This involved a mile-long tunnel under the city and the Patapsco River. A 600 volt direct current was used and the three little General Electric Company juice-jacks, each rated

Above left : New York, New Haven & Hartford Railroad pioneers the AC 11,000-volt, 25-cycle electrification dating from 1907. Note the triangular design of the overhead equipment.
Left : Great Northern Railway's electric locomotive races through the Cascade Mountains.
Right : Chicago, Milwaukee, St Paul & Pacific Railroad's 'Little Joe' electric locomotive at Deer Lodge.
Right inset : Pennsylvania Railroad's GG1 electric locomotives double-head a freight westbound through Eddystone.

at 1440 hp, were used to pull trains complete with idle steam locomotive into and out of Mount Royal station.

The classic case of the city ordinance forbidding the use of steam within its limits was New York's Grand Central Terminal. In 1903 the city's legislature passed an Act prohibiting the use after 1908 of steam locomotives south of the Harlem River. By 1907, all trains, including the high-and-mighty Twentieth Century Limited, began to be electrically hauled from Harmon, 20 miles out. This was also a third rail DC operation and is still in operation. Incidentally, a few of the original 1-D-1 (now 2-D-2) locomotives are still in service on Conrail; this longevity is typical of electric power.

Throughout the history of electrification, two rival systems have held their own. Direct current was the first, with, in general, a more expensive distribution system and simpler locomotives. Second came alternating current, with cheaper wiring but more expensive locomotives. Only recently has the matter been resolved by the development of a solid state conversion device (the thyristor – a relative of the transistor) whereby one can conveniently have an AC power supply with a DC motor on the locomotive. The first AC electrification in North America was on the New York, New Haven – Hartford Railroad completed by Westinghouse (whose speciality was AC, just as GEC preferred DC) in 1907. This used an 11,000 volt low-frequency overhead system that was used by a number of lines, but on the New Haven the locomotives were also equipped to run into Grand Central on a DC third rail.

Below : The Milwaukee Railroad's No E4, one of the famous 1-B-D + D-B-1 bi-polar electric locomotives.

Above right: One of the first locomotives built for the Milwaukee RR : 1-B-B + 1-B-B + B-B-1 No E41 for 3000 volts DC.

However, nothing in the nature of an electrified main route was seen until, in 1914, the Chicago, Milwaukee, St Paul & Pacific began their five-year-old transcontinental route to Seattle. By 1918 a total of 646 of the 1780 miles between St Paul and Seattle was under the wires. There were two separate sections, with a gap of 235 miles between them; the first went from Harlowton, Montana west to Avery, Idaho and the second from Othello to Tacoma, Washington. Ultimately 902 miles of contact wire, 22 electric sub-stations and 116 locomotives were in use, fueled by so called 'white coal', that is, current generated by water power. Amongst them were the 'Kings of the Rails', the five famous 'bi-polars', delivered by General Electric (the Milwaukee used 3000 volts DC) of the 1-B-D-D-B-1 wheel arrangement. They were called bi-polar because of the 12 special slow-speed gearless motors that were used, mounted directly on the axle. At 521,000 lbs they were, by present day standards, a little heavy for their power

of 3480 hp (a modern European locomotive of that rating would weigh less than half this), but they could move a 1000-ton train up 2.2 percent grades in the Cascade Mountains at 25 mph. They survived into the days of domes and streamliners, as well as colorful liveries, to match the new Olympian Hiawatha trains introduced after World War II. One is exhibited in the St Louis museum of transport and many thousands exist in model form. Alas, the whole of the Milwaukee electrification has now followed the bi-polars into history; like the steam engine, it was ousted by the diesel. It had originally cost $23 million, an enormous sum for the period, but by 1925 had not only paid for itself but also accumulated $12 million over and above this in estimated savings over steam traction.

With these facts in mind, the mighty Pennsylvania Railroad announced, in the unpropitious year of 1928, that the time had come to go electric. Only a financial Colossus could have proceeded with the most ambitious electrification project ever undertaken in the USA during the appalling depression era of 1929–1938. By the end of this period all the PRR main lines east of Harrisburg – a total of 670 route miles and 2200 track miles – were under the wires. The system used was the low-frequency (25 cycle) AC one developed on the New Haven.

This time five units no longer sufficed to protect the passenger workings; an equally handsome celebrated design called the GG1 was produced, of which eventually 139 were in use. The huge volume of work was shared by GEC (for once taking an AC order), Westinghouse, Baldwin's and the PRR's own Altoona

Above left : The Milwaukee Railroad's 'Little Joe' 2-D-D-2 No E 20 was originally built for the Soviet Union circa 1946 but the onset of the Cold War prevented delivery. Left : The Virginian Rail-road's twin-unit electric locomotive is used on a short but steep line. Above : Pennsylvania Railroad's famous GG1 2-C-C-2 No 4868 poses with the stainless steel Congressional Express.

WARNING
KEEP OFF
TOP AND SIDE
OF CAR

New York Central Railroad's No 4040 approaches Buffalo, New York's terminal. Inset top: Seaboard Air Line's early electromotive diesel unit. Inset bottom: Union Pacific Railroad's hood-unit diesel locomotive.

shops. In 40 years the GG1s have not become dated either in appearance or performance and today they are among Amtrak's most capable and reliable trains. Sadly, their days are running out, for the North-East Corridor line on which they operate is overdue for renewal of the power supply and it is unthinkable that the standard industrial supply frequency should not be used. However, Amtrak has some new prototype electric locomotives in service.

The other railroad giants (Union Pacific, Santa Fe, Southern Pacific, Southern Railway and Canadian Pacific) have looked at electrification but gone no further. One problem is that conversion to electric traction means total commitment. With 'dieselization,' if traffic falls, the most expensive part of the investment, the locomotives, are at least saleable elsewhere. Thus no common-carrier railroad in North America has taken the plunge. We may note, however, that a new electric coal-hauling railroad in Ohio, called the Muskingum Electric Railroad, has been built by the American Electric Power Company. It was electrified as a test-bed for the latest concepts in high-voltage, industrial frequency, AC electrification – using DC motors – and started operation in 1968. Another in Arizona has followed.

Two points remain; in the first place, most diesels are more correctly described as electric locomotives of the self-generating type, their wheels being driven by electric motors for which a diesel engine and dynamo generates current. Thus, a changeover to electric traction involves little alteration – merely a big simplification – to the locomotives.

Finally, as the world's oil supplies dwindle, it is not so much a question of whether to electrify but rather when to electrify; the period that may elapse before this point is reached is measurable not in years but in decades. In the meantime, the diesel locomotive remains in charge.

The diesel conquest of North America was remarkable both for its completeness and its speed. It started with the first successful road diesel on Canadian National in 1928. Before that only low-powered diesel switchers and railcars had been in service. By 1938 production units were available, by 1948 steam locomotive construction had virtually ceased and by 1958 it was all over, except for a few minor pockets of resistance. Apart from pleasure lines, the North-East Corridor electrified route is now the only non-diesel operation of any size that remains in North America.

The concept was correct from the start. The two Canadian National units used the diesel engine which was an English Beardmore adapted from submarine practice which drove a dynamo. Current from this was used to drive electric motors geared to the wheels. In essence the design was no different to most of today's, an electric locomotive that carries its own power plant. The second feature, one which also appears in most modern diesels, was that the units, each of 1300 hp, could be multiple-coupled to make one 2600 hp locomotive for heavy trains, while they could be used singly for lighter ones. Despite their promise, the units languished through lack of funds in the depression years, but one survived to

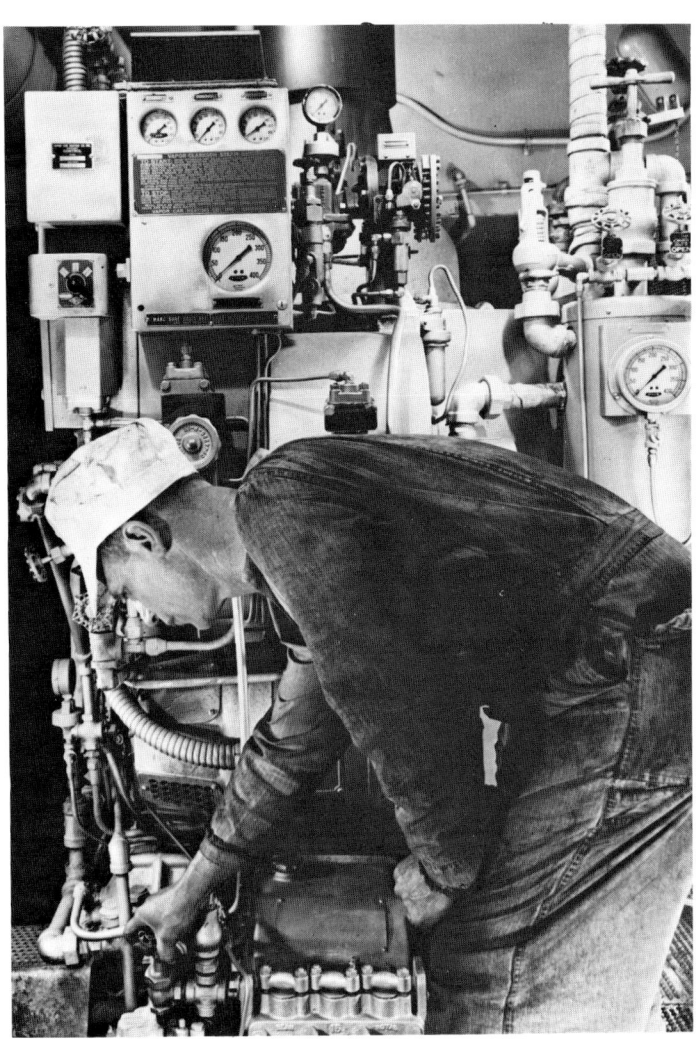

operate – with a new engine – through and after World War II, being finally retired in 1946.

It is relevant to mention that the problem with an internal combustion engine, gasoline or diesel, is that it only delivers torque when running. Loco-motion, however, needs a strong torque when starting so, means have to be found to couple a running engine to a stationary wheel, without breaking, bursting or burning any of the mechanism. Mechanical, electrical, hydraulic and pneumatic solutions have been tried, but the electric one is that which has so far prevailed in North America for powers of 1000 horsepower and over. The steam locomotive does not suffer from this drawback; when steam is admitted to the cylinders, the push on the pistons directly propels the train.

From 1922 onwards, a small firm called the Electro-motive Company of La Grange, Illinois had supplied some 500 small gasoline-electric railcars, known as Doodlebugs, for light passenger services in numerous railroads. In 1930 General Motors acquired both Electro-motive and its engine supplier, the Winton Engine Company.

Far left: Amtrak's new class E-60 electric loco-motive.
Left: Diesel traction is very different from steam. Here a diesel technician makes an examination.

Bottom: Southern Pacific's big guns await assignments at Los Angeles' terminal.

A streamlined Union
Pacific freight is pulled by
four units. The scrubby
area in the foreground is
a pile of cinders emitted
from thousands of Big
Boys, Challengers and
other steam engines of
days gone by.
Inset : Pile on the horsepower! Four general pur-
pose hood-unit diesels
running 'in multiple'
leave Alyth yard, Cal-
gary, Alberta.

Left: An early Great Northern Railway four-unit freight diesel – the one that conquered America – pulls a solid train of reefers near Blacktail, Montana. A three-unit helper is pushing at the rear making 9400 hp in all.
Bottom: The Union Pacific Railroad's M-10001, built of aluminium alloy in 1934, was one of the US's earliest diesel streamliners and was later renamed the City of Portland. It was liveried bright yellow with brown and scarlet trim.

With this experience and backing, Electro-motive were asked to power a remarkable Pullman-built articulated, three-car, all-aluminium, streamlined train for Union Pacific. It was powered by a spark-plug V-12 engine, rated at 400 hp and, having the remarkably low weight of 85 tons and excellent aerodynamic qualities, managed 110 mph on test. So, on 12 February 1934, the streamline era began. After a 12,000-mile coast-to-coast tour, it went into service as the City of Salina.

The inflammability and high cost of even low-grade gasoline encouraged the use of an improved diesel engine for traction use. At that time, typical diesels weighed 80 lb for each horsepower developed. The General Motors' target of 20 lb/hp was achieved in 1933 with a two-stroke, 600 hp, eight cylinder in-line design.

The first railroad to realize the potential of the diesel, and back their judgment with the order book, was the Chicago, Burlington & Quincy. The Burlington ordered a three-car set, powered by this 600 hp engine and with seats for a total of 72 passengers. Though a fairly modest affair by later standards, the *Pioneer Zephyr* train soon showed its paces by achieving an average speed of 77.5 mph on its inaugural run of 1015 miles from Denver to Chicago on 26 May 1935, thereby earning itself a sure place in railway history by becoming the first of the nation's diesel-powered high-speed trains. Union Pacific also followed up the City of Salina with a larger six-car diesel set. As the City of Portland this train ran a regular service between Portland and Chicago, making some remarkable performances. On speed trials it notched up a top speed of 120 mph and an average over a 60-mile run of 102.8 mph. Its most memorable record-breaking achievement was a transcontinental coast-to-coast haul of 3193 miles which it completed in 56 hours and 55 minutes.

Several more of these integral streamlined trains were put into service, each longer and more powerful than the last. By 1936 the Burlington's Denver Zephyr had (thanks to multiple engines) 3000 hp and UP's City of Denver 2400 hp. The problem was that the motive power was inseparably linked to its train and could not easily be used for other trains or cut out for repairs. Electro-motive, therefore, went on to develop a straight road locomotive and, in conjunction with General Electric, produced a prototype pair, each unit with two 900 hp engines, making 3600 hp in all.

Baltimore & Ohio, showing the passage of over one hundred years had not quenched its pioneering spirit, ordered the first production unit, but Santa Fe stole the limelight by having two to inaugurate the now legendary de-luxe all Pullman Super-Chief train on its weekly run from Chicago to Los Angeles.

In 1937, Electro-motive began marketing the E-1, a standard diesel passenger locomotive in two versions; there were cab units with, as the name implies,

a control cab at one end and booster units, without cabs, used to make up the units into locomotives of higher power. By 1938, a modified E-1 called the E-6 was sufficiently in demand for mass-production to begin. Power was increased to 2000 hp per unit. The first company to buy this locomotive was the Seaboard Air Line for its Orange Blossom Special from Washington to Miami. SAL's configuration was cab-booster-cab, giving a double-ended 6000 hp locomotive. Each unit had two three-axle trucks of which only the outer axles were powered. The following year a demonstrator four-unit freight locomotive of 5400 hp was produced of cab-booster-booster-cab formation. This machine, No 103, carried out an 83,000 mile nation-wide demonstration run, showing that it could haul any load that steam could handle and that it was more than extremely reliable. Although at 900,000 lb, No 103 weighed considerably more than any steam locomotive ever built, because this load was carried on 36 axles, the engine could go anywhere a freightcar could. In contrast, the biggest steam powered engines were restricted to the principal main lines. Furthermore, in all this journeying, 103 needed very few stops for servicing and was normally available for traffic at the press of a button, in very strong contrast to the typical steam locomotive was well on the move. However, damage very much easier to operate and for this the Electromotive Division of General Motors must take most of the credit.

In a freight train, the couplings between adjacent cars contain a small amount of slack and in a long train, this adds up to a significant amount. In steam days, slack was used to advantage in getting a train on the move; for the first few feet only a few cars would have to be started and by the time the last ones were violently jerked into motion the locomotive was well on the move. However, damage often occurred at the rear of the train. A diesel on the other hand, has, for a given power, a much higher starting pull than a steam locomotive, so there is no need to use slack as an aid to starting, hence, less damage.

It is the writer's opinion that it was these operational factors rather than economic ones that led to the diesel taking over. The diesel was press-button power, could go anywhere, was easy to drive and, by regarding the units as building blocks, could be made up into a size of locomotive to suit any train. Where any fair and scientific comparison was made between steam and diesel, the total economics of systems were almost identical although *individual* items in the balance sheet were very different.

Below left : Experimental (and short-lived) gas turbine locomotive used by Chicago & North Western Railway in 1952. Bottom right : A 6000-hp diesel locomotive pulling the then new Olympian Hiawatha speedliner. Below : A parade of early diesel-electric power surrounds a lone steam locomotive.

For example, while fuel for a diesel cost one-third that for steam, the initial cost and amortization of a diesel was, in contrast (while facilities for mass-production of steam power still existed), three times as much. And although still an expensive proposition, the maintenance and repairs of steam locomotives due to their simplicity was relatively cheap compared to diesels. Of course, where steam operation had become very run down, this was not so and it was certainly much easier to borrow money on the surety of mobile assets like diesels rather than on immobile ones like new steam repair and servicing facilities.

Be that as it may, once the war had finished the figures tell their own story.

Units Ordered

Year	Steam	Diesel
1944	326	750
1945	115	800
1946	86	950
1947	69	1900
1948	86	2850
1949	57	1950
1950	12	2400

By the end of the war, diesels had completed their takeover. It remained only for other manufacturers and traditional locomotive builders to enter the scene; for the universal road-switcher to appear; the old camel-back arrangement to return when cabs and boosters were superseded by hood units which allowed engineers and firemen to look out in both directions. High-powered single-unit diesels were tried and discarded more than once; the gas-turbine made a valiant bid for supremacy on Union Pacific, but in vain.

One of the innovations which was adopted was the radio-controlled slave unit which could be cut in down the train in situations where there was a danger of the drawbars being pulled out if all the power was placed at the head of the train. In passenger units, the steam train heating boiler is giving way to a winding on the main generator to provide electric power for heating and air-conditioning.

As the golden jubilee of the diesel road locomotive approaches, nothing fundamental is found to have changed and no serious rival is in sight. No doubt the diesel will continue to rule the railroads of North America until the oil-wells dry up.

Below : The current general-purpose diesel. Note 'hood-unit' cab arrangement.
Bottom : The gas-turbine electric units of 8500 hp replaced the Big Boys.

Right : Detroit, Toledo & Ironton's Electromotive Division Class GP 38, Flatrock, Michigan.
Right inset : Southern Pacific switchers, Oakland, California, 1970.

LINES AND EQUIPMENT

At the end of 1830, there were 23 miles of railroad in the United States; by 1850 9000, by 1870 53,000 and by the turn of the century 193,000. In 1887 alone, almost 13,000 miles of railroad were added to the network. The current figure is around the 200,000 mile mark. Since the land is crisscrossed with natural obstacles, rivers, hills, swamps and mountains, inimical to the construction of railroads, it follows that this construction task was an immense one.

Most of this track was laid on grades dictated by the natural lie of the land on cuts or fills. In the early days mule- and horsepower was used, but machines have taken over by degrees. The first primitive steam-shovels eventually developed into the construction man's current comprehensive armory of earth-moving equipment. On every construction project there comes a point where the boring of a tunnel becomes cheaper than a cutting, but bridges were always more prominent than tunnels in the American scene. Railroad builders in North America had, perhaps, greater freedom in their choice of route than their European counterparts, since they tended to be creating new communities rather than serving existing ones; hence the relative absence of tunnels as surveyors usually could choose routes that did not need them. The crossing of the great rivers could not, however, be avoided.

Even if the longest American tunnel is twelfth in length on the world scale the longest-ever, the current longest, the longest existing, and the longest-

Left : Southern Pacific passenger trains board the train ferry to cross the Straits of Carquinez north of San Francisco. The wharf at Porta Costa had an adjustable apron.

Preceding spread: Southern Pacific's The City of San Francisco crosses the then new Martinez-Benicia Bridge across San Francisco Bay, 1940.

ever single-span railroad bridges are all in North America. The longest-ever bridge was the timber trestle built by Southern Pacific across the Great Salt Lake in 1904. It was 20 miles long but over the years has gradually been replaced by an embankment. The object was to avoid 78 miles of sharply curved and graded road round the north shore (which included the place called Promontory, of golden spike fame) and replace them with 50 miles of direct track. It amply justified itself by savings in operating costs.

Several railroads (including SP) use the Huey P Long bridge over the Mississippi River at New Orleans. This steel and concrete bridge was completed in 1938 and is 4.4 miles long. The greatest span is 790 feet. While on the subject of Southern Pacific, this railroad was responsible in 1950 for building another very long bridge across the Straits of Martinez – an arm of San Francisco Bay – to replace a train ferry operation, which had been a bugbear of the Overland Route since its inception.

Right: Steam locomotive No 12 crosses a trestle bridge on a narrow-gauge (three-foot) sugar line in Maui, Hawaii.
Below left: Wooden trestle bridges such as this example on the Canadian Pacific in the Rockies were a characteristic feature of North American railroad construction in rugged terrain in the early days. After a short life, these timber trestles would be replaced with easier-to-maintain fills.

The largest span railway bridge existing in the world today is the cantilever bridge at Quebec over the St Lawrence River carrying the Canadian National Railway. The span is 1800 feet and it was opened in 1917 after many vicissitudes including a failure of one of the main cantilevers in 1907 and the dropping of the suspended span while being lifted into position in 1916. The longest span which has ever carried railroad trains is the San Francisco Bay suspension bridge with two 2310-foot spans, but the interurban trains which used it no longer run. The suspension bridge principle is not normally considered suitable for carrying concentrated railroad loadings.

Top right: Great Northern's Empire Builder steams across the Gassman Coulee Ravine on a steel trestle in North Dakota.
Left: The White Pass & Yukon Railway's rotary unit crosses the High Level Bridge over Dead Horse Gulch.
Left above: Only 25 miles from Skagway, Alaska, the rotary unit of the White Pass & Yukon Railway continues to clear out the Fraser Loop.

Of course, the majority of bridges on any railway are small and formed from plain steel, concrete or even timber beams. They carry the tracks across streams, highways, other railroads and vice versa. Even double-decker bridges are not unknown. A series of short spans are very much cheaper than one long one, so if conditions permit, it is usually economic to have intermediate supports. The classic example is the type of bridge which opened up the American West, the timber trestle. Usually, ample supplies of good timber were close at hand and, since this form of construction lends itself to rapid erection with unskilled hand labor, trestles were often preferred to the alternative of a fill. The only drawback is an excessive maintenance cost. Thus, we find railroads faced with early replacement, either by tipping a fill or by replacing the timber trestle with one of steel.

Stone arched bridges, either over or under the railway, which are so common in older countries, can be found in quantity in the eastern States. Maintenance costs are very low and, moreover, the fill over the top of the arch consolidates with time and lends an increased strength to the structure. On the other hand, deep and firm foundations as well as skilled labor are required.

Arches made of steel or concrete are often used now instead of girder or cantilever bridges. This kind of arch can be regarded as a special case where a deep girder is helped to carry the load by being

Above : Chesapeake &
Ohio RR, Seaboard RR
and Southern RR cross
each other on girder
double-decker bridges in
Richmond, Virginia.
Right bottom : Three
locomotives drag a train
formed of only eight
wooden cars up the
original 4 percent grade
of the Kicking Horse Pass.

pressed inwards low down at the ends. A noble one
is Canadian Pacific's Stoney Creek Bridge in British
Colombia.

The scarcity of tunnels in North America has
been duly noted; some were needed for the process of
upgrading the routes – by downgrading the grades –
which took place during the early years of the century. A famous example is Great Northern's 7.75 mile
Cascade Tunnel diversion, which in 1910 replaced
43 miles of difficult grades with 34 miles of easier
ones. Denver & Rio Grande Western's six-mile
Moffat Tunnel on the Dotsero to Orestod cut-off
effectively reduced the distance between Denver and
Salt Lake City by 65 miles.

Sometimes this improvement of grade had to be
paid for by additional distance and such exotic
devices as helicoidal tunnels like the famous
Field Hill on Canadian Pacific. CP originally crossed
the range via the Kicking Horse Pass with grades of
4.4 percent. In 1910, after 25 years of hideously

traumatic operation, a new alignment involving two spiral tunnels was constructed with a ruling grade of 2.2 percent. Under the new conditions, two locomotives could haul 40 percent more than four could previously. All this was achieved at a cost of an additional four miles. In steam days, conditions inside the spirals were rather severe and hobos 'riding the rods' on freight trains used to alight at the entrances, climb on foot to the exit some distance higher up and wait for the train there, the train crew no doubt wishing they could do it too. It is worth noting that in really steep places legs can have the edge on trains.

This Canadian Pacific experience illustrates how ruinously expensive it is to run a cheaply built railroad; also why, since Field Hill was only one example, so many railroads spent so many millions of dollars from 1880 even to the present day, on line relocations of this kind.

Left : The Canadian, Canadian Pacific's transcontinental train, crosses the arched steel Stoney Creek Bridge in British Columbia.
Below : A Canadian Pacific seemingly endless freight train crosses under itself as it passes through the spiral tunnel built to ease the grade of the Kicking Horse Pass in British Columbia.

One of the most remarkable feats of railroad engineering in the USA was a glorious folly that crossed the sea for 114 miles, not to reach a destination, but merely to shorten the sea passage between Florida and Cuba, then an important commerce and tourist link. The Key West Extension of the Florida East Coast Railway, completed in 1912, included 17 miles of bridging. There are 20 miles of embankment in shallow water and the remainder is laid on the coral reefs known as Keys. In 1936 a hurricane ended any railway operations, but the right of way was subsequently reconstructed as a road. At more than one place lifting spans had to be provided in order to clear a channel for navigation; such a feature is common wherever railroads have to cross navigable water. The movable span can be arranged to lift horizontally or, more commonly, to pivot at one end or even to swing.

However, anyone who has faced the task of maintaining a railroad soon realizes that the spec-

117

Left: A Norfolk & Western straight locomotive shed – such tidiness was untypical of the steam era.
Above: A steam rotary snowplow clears the line for the White Pass & Yukon Railway.
Below left: A Mikado passes over the steel trestle and girder Cedar Grove Viaduct in New Jersey on the Erie.

tacular forms a very small part of the problem. The prime responsibility is to keep the trains on the track, which means that spikes and ties should hold the rails to gauge and, moreover, to a reasonable standard of line and level. On the class I railroads of North America there are some 400,000 miles of track; this means 350,000,000 rails, 1,200,000,000 ties and so on which need to be kept in good order.

The financial problems which affect certain railroads are more than evident to the track maintenance forces. Lines which should rate new heavy rails have to continue with older and lighter, worn ones. There is no chance of renewing suspect timber ties wholesale and supporting them on a deep bed of crushed stone ballast, all of which needs be done if the railroad is to be adequately maintained.

The track itself has evolved slowly from light rails weighing 30 lbs to the yard (or less) fastened with four spikes to untreated wooden ties. The ties are now treated and baseplates under rails weighing 132 lbs/yd (occasionally more) help to spread the loading. Reinforced (pre-stressed) concrete sleepers

are now used by the best people, often in conjunction with continuously welded rail, in order to eliminate joint bars and their associated problems. However much the track material and roadbed is improved, on any line where trains are more than an occasional event, constant vigilance is required if wrecks are to be avoided.

At all times possible tree- and rock-falls have to be looked for not to mention such things as unauthorized excavations close to the track which might weaken it. In bad weather or when rivers are in spate, vulnerable places where wash-outs might occur have to be watched. The big structures get VIP treatment from the top brass of the Engineering Departments, and so very seldom are a headache for those closer to the ground, on whom the main burden of keeping the trains running necessarily falls. The train maintenance crews must do the best they can under existing circumstances.

Before trains could be run on the tracks at all, depots, terminals and systems of operation had to be created. Passenger depots ranged from the discarded boxcar dumped by the side of the tracks up to Grand

Above: Canadian National Railway's locomotive cleaning facilities not only add to the appearance of the trains but help to maintain them as well. Below: This wayside depot at Banff, Alberta is typical in its architecture but not in its setting.

Left: The exterior of New York City's Grand Central Station.
Right: The Interior of New York's Grand Central from the main concourse looking towards the stairs.
Far right: A pleasant change is the mission style architecture found in Union Station in Los Angeles.
Bottom left and right: The interior and exterior of Union Station in Chicago.
Below center: Union Station in Washington in the early years after the war. This station is now the focal point of the new Washington Metro.

Central Station in New York City, the most valuable single property in Manhattan. Grand Central was opened in 1913. It replaced another station which itself only dated from 1898. When the original Grand Central was constructed, it was intended to accommodate the growth of traffic for 50 years. However, in less than ten years it was completely inadequate and total reconstruction had to be undertaken. There was one additional degree of freedom which the architects of the new station possessed – a direct result of the advent of electric traction, introduced in 1906. This time they did not have to worry about smoke and after the tracks had been laid, building sites were available for sale at the street level above. Forty-eight tracks were provided, 31 on an upper level for long distance trains and 17 below for commuter trains. Loops on each level were provided so that a train could arrive and leave the station without reversing. The architecture, exterior and interior would not have disgraced Imperial Rome. Every kind of shop was present including restaurants, a post office, art gallery, gymnasium and even tennis courts, a theater and a hospital. 'A city within a city', it was called. The cost was $65,000,000 in the dollars of 1913.

The suburban trains still run in and out in their hundreds each working day, but in 1977 there are only eight pairs of long distance trains daily to use the 31 upper level tracks provided for this traffic. The great hall which leads to them is, in consequence, becoming a little shabby.

Stations in other important cities tell a similar story. As for passenger depots in lesser places, the trains simply do not call there any more except perhaps in the remoter and still roadless parts of Canada. The other exceptions are those fortunate places which still have rail commuter service plus a few on museum lines.

The next most interesting groups of railway facilities for the general observer are locomotive terminals. Diesel servicing is not too different from that of the familiar automobile, while that of electrics is fairly negligible. However, attending to steam locomotives was very different. Requirements such as coaling (coaling plants represent an early triumph of machines over men), ash disposal by the ton, washing out boilers and the rest meant something much more elaborate. The sheds usually took the well-known form of a roundhouse, with covered stalls radiating from a turntable, itself a massive and complex contrivance. The arrangement was workable until something put the turntable out of action, when a whole depot-full of power would get locked in. Nevertheless, this form was almost universal and as a name it persists today, and is often applied even to a diesel facility laid out as a straight shed.

Freight yards, in which cars are sorted and marshaled into trains, have also changed over the years, but, of course, show progress rather than decline. The original method, still used in smaller locations, would be for a switching engine to draw a string of cars from one track and then, one or more at a time, kick them into the yard track appropriate for their new destination. For many years now,

freight sorting yards of any size have been laid out as gravity or hump yards. Strings of cars to be sorted are pushed slowly over a steep hump in the track. The uncoupling levers are lifted between pairs of cars as they pass. In other words, as a car passes over the hump it separates itself from its neighbor behind and runs down into the appropriate one of perhaps 40 sorting sidings, which fan out immediately beyond the hump. In a second or two the next car will separate itself in succession, but during this interval there is time to reset the points to take this next car into its appropriate siding. Having got the cars rolling nicely down off the hump, aided by a general gravitational fall provided on the sorting grid, the next problem is to stop them. In modern yards this

is done by rail brakes or retarders, which grab the wheels as they go by. The amount of braking necessary depends on a variety of things – the direction and strength of the wind, the weight and 'rollability' of the car and the distance it has to go before meeting the previous one in that siding. Computerization has had disappointing results and the human 'hump' operator generally still plies his trade.

Computerization of other aspects of yard and operating work has, in contrast, been very successful. The problem is, of course, to keep control of the tens of thousands of cars moving on a large railroad. Foremost amongst the systems is one developed – after some traumatic near-failures – by the Southern Pacific Railroad which is called TOPS, the Total Operations Processing System. This has been adopted by two of the other largest railroads on the continent, Burlington Northern and Canadian National (who call it TRACS) and also – to show its adaptibility to very different circumstances – by British Railways. Penn Central was on the point of taking it when bankruptcy intervened in 1970. TOPS keeps a record in a central computer of where each car (and locomotive) is, its destination, its contents, its type, its consignee and consignor and many other things. Against each location and against each train is recorded a list of the appropriate cars. Each local office has punched cards and printed output for its records and for each car and locomotive in its territory there is a punched card.

Operating men can make enquiries ranging from simple requests for the details of a particular vehicle to a general enquiry concerning wide flows of traffic or the availability of particular types of car. In this way management is able to control and manage to the best advantage the main part of its business, the mass movement of freight.

An interesting feature is that an ICC requirement in the late 1960s laid down that all cars interchanged between railroads should be equipped for automatic car identification. Colored encoded strips are fixed to car sides and these can be read by ACI readers placed at suitable points along the tracks. Except in the case of some specialized applications, however,

results have been a little disappointing. This is partly because the coded labels tend to be affected by snow and dirt, and also because systems such as TOPS need to record so much more than just the number.

Nothing has so far been discussed regarding the principles of making up layouts. The plain turnout is the commonest component; they are known by a number which represents the angle at which the rails cross, expressed as, say, 1 in 10. This would be a No 10 turnout. The sharper the angle, the slower the speed at which it can be safely traversed but sharper turnouts are shorter and hence cheaper. A freight yard would be laid out with No 10 or No 8 turnouts, while a fast running junction in a main line might rate one as flat as a No 20. The angles of diamond crossings, where one line crosses another on the level, are usually specified in degrees and, in addition, combination turnouts and diamonds, known as slip points, are used (with some reluctance, because complications always cause problems) when space is limited. More, however, can be learned about the principles involved in a few minutes spent setting up a child's model railway than in pages of discourse.

Infrequently used points or switches are worked by hand levers but others are normally worked from an interlocking tower when concentrated or remotely when situated by themselves or in small numbers. Fixed signals, either semaphore or colored light, are connected up in the same way. The term interlocking means that they cannot be put to 'all-clear' without the switches being correctly aligned and once

Top left: A hump operator at work in an automated hump yard.
Bottom left: Aerial photograph of the Alyth automated hump yard, Calgary, Alberta.
Above: In this bird's eye view of the Pocatello yard of the Union Pacific RR, the retarders which automatically brake cars rolling off the hump can be seen to the rear of the turnouts in the foreground.
Below: The interlocking mission tower controls the approaches to Union Station in Los Angeles.

signals are in the 'all-clear' position, switches cannot be moved.

From the first, it was recognized that trains, unlike horse-drawn stages, could not normally stop on demand. For one thing, they went much faster and, for another, being confined to rails they could not dodge. Experience was gained the hard way, but eventually standardized operating rules evolved, by which a gentleman known as the dispatcher is given absolute authority over movements on a particular section of line. Trains normally run to a fixed time-table, making the 'meets' specified therein, but any extra trains or extra sections of a booked train or variations in booked crossing points are dealt with by the dispatcher. After deciding how to handle them, he issues train orders by telegraph to the station agents concerned. One copy is handed to the engineer of any train affected, by the railroad agent at the point concerned, as well as another to the conductor. There is usually a three-position signal at each station, now semaphore but originally a ball-signal – hence the term 'highball'. The signal aspects give indications as follows:

Vertical or right up – full speed ahead, no orders
Diagonal or half-way – pick up orders as you pass
Horizontal or low down – Stop

A train order will instruct the train crew, for example, to run to a specified place and go inside for, say, the extra No 487 east. The place where the meet is to happen need not necessarily be manned and, on reaching it, the train will turn the switch for the siding for the train to go in, after which someone at the rear will line it up for the main. Then, the train will not move until the 487 east does appear, clearly marked by its number in an illuminated sign-case at the front on either side.

Many railroad lines in America are still worked in this way, but the norm for main lines is a system called continuous train control or CTC. With this, the line is fully signaled and signals, together with the siding switches, are remotely controlled from what had once been the dispatchers office; the people there can now tell engineers what to do immediately and directly. Train orders are still used, but to a much lesser degree, confined more to special items like emergency slow orders which cannot be put across by the fixed signals. Where double lines are not (as is often the case) worked as two single ones, the problem of meets does not arise and the signals can work automatically in each direction, not clearing until the previous train has moved out.

Cab signaling is used in various forms by various companies, notably the old Pennsylvania which many years ago began giving engineers a continuous indication right in the cab of the state of the road ahead, using a system of variable frequency current in the rails. Radio communication with and between train crews is now commonplace and contributes much to the safety of operation.

Finally, a chapter on behind-the-scenes railroading, would not be complete if mention were not made of the office work which makes it all possible. Each car moved needs its way-bill; every man employed needs his pay-check, every nut-and-bolt, cup-and-saucer and can of oil needs to be bought, stored and issued; timetables and returns need compilation; takings have to be counted; and customers have to be wooed if business is to continue at all.

Above : Locomotive
roundhouse and turn-
table at Turcot,
Montreal, Quebec.
Far left : The driver of a
wartime Santa Fe
Railroad freight headed
by four diesel-electric
units totaling 5400 hp
picks up operating orders
from the telegraph office
at West Winslow yard,
Arizona.
Left : A very modern
automated hump yard
control panel.

PASSENGER AND FREIGHT CARS

PASSENGER AND FREIGHT CARS

In 1877 a newspaper reporter on a 'freeloading' transcontinental rail trip west ventured out of the luxurious security of his millionaire host's private hotel car to take a look at conditions on the rest of the train. In a first-class car he found: a consumptive invalid bent double in a paroxysm of coughing; 'four parties, invisible but palpable to the touch, are wrestling in the agonies of the toilet behind closely buttoned curtains and trampling on the toes of passers-by. Two young lovers are exchanging endearments in a remote corner. Who could bear these things with perfect equanimity? Who could rise under the close personal scrutiny of 29 distinct homicides?'

If that was first-class accommodation . . . 'What about the ordinary passenger car', he wrote, 'wherein working men and working women – the miners, gold seekers, trappers, hunters and queer backwoodsfolk – congregate, all packed like sardines in a box? It is pathetic to see the vain attempts to improvise out of their two or three feet of space a comfortable sleeping

Above: An old style, day-night convertible Pullman between the wars. On the left of the center gangway is seating for daytime use and on the right of this Canadian National Railway's car the conductor has let down the upper berths and made up the beds for night use.
Far left : Interior of an old-fashioned traditional day-coach of the Milwaukee & Northern Railroad.
Left : This lounge-observation car typical of the first decade of this century with an open observation platform was operated by Canadian Pacific Railways.
Preceding spread : Interior of a colonial sleeping-car on the Canadian Pacific Railway in its early days.

space for some sick girl or feeble old person. Every seat has its occupant, by night as well as day, a congregation of aching spines.'

Having expended so much sympathy, it is probably as well the reporter did not encounter the third-and even lower class of passenger – the $40-ticket emigrant. He would not have found them on his train however, for being no more than freight to the railroads they were treated as such and emigrant cars were hitched to mixed freight trains to make their slow, exasperating way west, spending much of their journey in sidings.

Second-class passengers did, at least, have upholstered seats to sleep on, albeit upright. Emigrants were provided with nothing more than wooden

Right: *Pioneer* was Pullman's first sleeping car built in 1865 at a cost of over $20,000. The interior was finished in polished black walnut, crimson French plush and equipped with pure linen, chandeliers with candles, mirrors and marble washstands.
Below: This dining car of the late 1920s operated on the Washington-Baltimore-Chicago Capitol Limited of the Baltimore & Ohio RR, and sported reproduction Hepplewhite chairs, Sheraton sideboards and Georgian leaded windows.

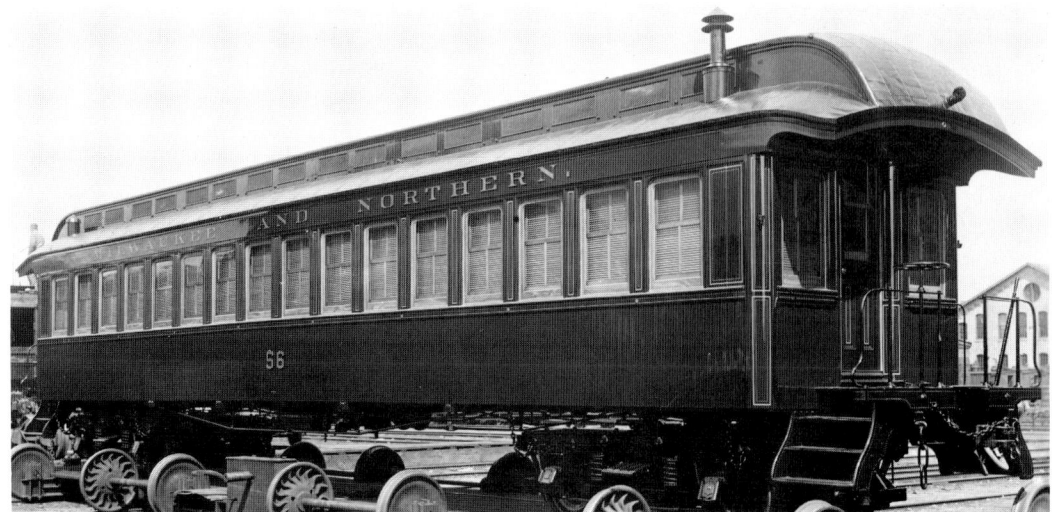

Left: The day coach of the Milwaukee & Northern Railroad had a clerestory roof and an open-end gallery.
Right: A Canadian National Railway's dining car of the 1920s.

benches and were only lucky enough to sleep horizontally, if at all, when space allowed them to hire a sleeping board to bridge the gap between facing benches. Robert Louis Stevenson, then a minor travel writer and yet to make his name as a novelist, experienced the rigors of an emigrant train in 1879 and recalled his impressions of 'that long narrow wooden box, like a flat-roofed Noah's ark'. The wooden seats, he reported, were: 'too short for anything but a young child. Where there is scarce elbow room for two to sit, there will not be space enough for one to lie.'

Both cars and coaches were heated by wood-burning stoves and lit first by candle and then by oil – both features, in combination with all-wooden cars, putting passengers in constant danger of immolation in the event of a crash.

In half a century of rail travel, during which stupendous feats of engineering had enabled a continent to be bridged and locomotive design to make undreamed-of strides, coach facilities had hardly progressed since the first 'stage-coach' patterns were taken over by long, open carriages. For the well-heeled, however, it was a vastly different story. Luxury passenger car design had in the second half of the century reached a point where the degree of comfort on wheels which could be bought by those who could afford it was probably surpassed only by their own homes or the grandest hotels.

George Mortimer Pullman, whose name itself became synonymous with comfort at its utmost, began experimenting with sleeping cars in the 1850s and three early adaptations were being run on the Chicago & Alton Railroad by the end of the decade.

1859

"OLD No. 9" THE FIRST PULLMAN CAR The first Pullman sleeper, built 1859, was a reconstructed day coach, 40 feet long or about half the present length. Except wheels and axles, it was practically all wood. The roof was flat and so low a tall man was liable to bump his head. The seats were immovable; two small wood-burning stoves furnished heat. Lighted with candles, it had at each end a small toilet room large enough for one person, with tin wash basin in the open and water from the drinking faucet. There were ten upper and ten lower berths; mattresses and blankets, but no sheets. But it was the best yet.

1907

THE ALL-STEEL CAR APPEARS No other advance in car building made so much for safety, up to this date, as all-steel construction. Following the first experimental steel car, in 1907, the type was adopted in general service in 1910. Length 74 feet; full vestibule; 12 sections, drawing room and smoking room; steel sheathed outside; electric light from axle device; low pressure vapor heat system. Interiors were by this time becoming more quiet, moderate and tasteful, with plain mottled finish, green frieze plush upholstery and green carpets. This was the period of standardization.

1937

THE ROOMETTE CAR The Pullman Company's latest innovation in travel comfort is the Roomette car. Each Roomette is a small completely enclosed private room, containing one bed which folds into the wall at one end of the room and a sofa-seat for daytime service. In this car there are 18 Roomettes, each with complete toilet facilities, individually air-conditioned and separate control of heat and light. The car is of alloy steel construction, air-conditioned and contains all the modern appurtenances for modern Pullman travel comfort.

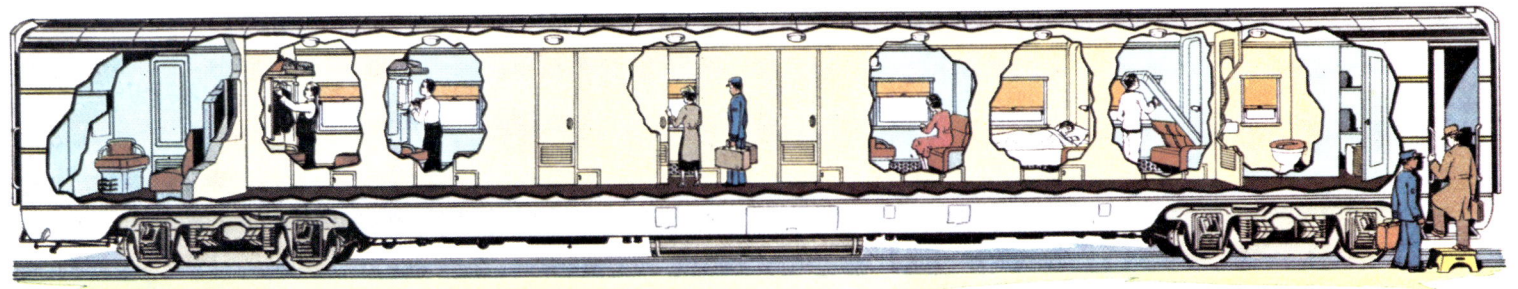

1876

THE STEADY MARCH OF PROGRESS CENTENNIAL YEAR—1876—opened a period of further progress. The car's length grew from 58 to 70 feet. Oil lamps superseded candles. Air brakes appeared, making for greater speed and safety. A hot water heating system replaced stoves and furnaces. Six-wheel trucks were definitely adopted and overhead tanks with gravity supply system afforded water. Interior finish was in walnut, with carving, inlaying and lacquer work characteristic of the period.

1929

AIR-CONDITIONING SYSTEM With the introduction of the first successfully operated air-conditioned sleeping car in 1929, the Pullman Company rapidly added this innovation in travel comfort to its equipment and by 1937 operated over 50% of all the air-conditioned passenger cars in the United States. The mechanical devices employed in air-conditioning indicated in the car are as follows:

1. INTAKES	6. HOLDOVER COIL	11. RECEIVING TANK	17. STANDBY MOTOR
2. FILTERS	7. DUCTS	12. DOUBLE PULLEY	18. TANK FOR AUXILIARY
3. BLOWERS	8. GRILLED OUTLETS	13. DRIVE BELTS	HOLDOVER SYSTEM
4. COOLING COIL OR	9. COMPRESSOR	14. BEVEL GEAR UNIT	19. COOLING COILS
EVAPORATOR	10. CONDENSER	15. DRIVE SHAFT	20. LOWER BERTH NOZZLE
5. HEATING RADIATOR		16. SPEED CONTROL	OUTLET

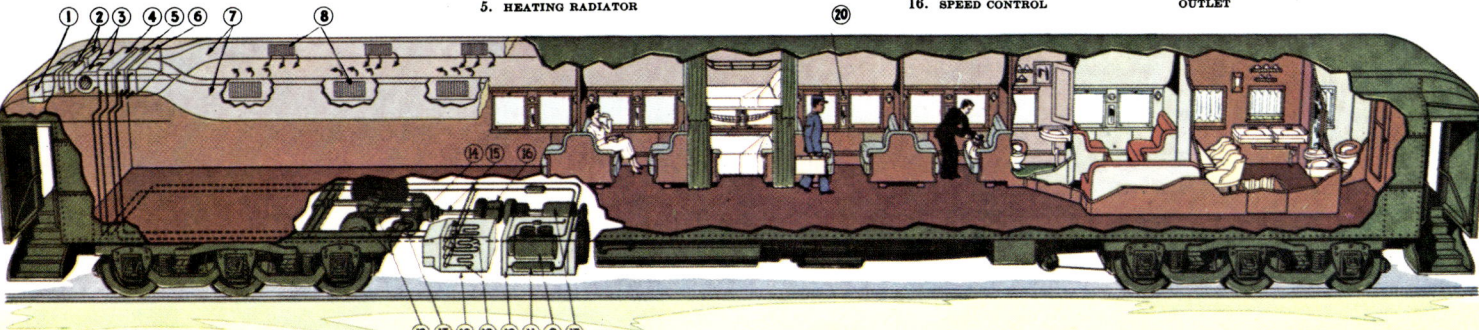

1942

DUPLEX-ROOMETTE This car gives Pullman passengers individual rooms and the comforts of a "hotel on wheels." The rooms, which are on two slightly varying floor levels, interlock, permitting Pullman to build 24 luxury accommodations in a single car. The roomy bed in the lower duplex slides under the floor of the adjacent room, which is two steps above aisle level. In the upper roomette, the bed swings up into the wall. The duplexes become private sitting rooms in daytime, contain their own lavatory and toilet, and heat, light and air conditioning are designed for the individual's personal control.

The first all-Pullman-built sleeping car, the *Pioneer*, appeared in 1864, incorporating all the features which became so familiar to first-class travelers in the late nineteenth and early twentieth centuries. The car, with the ubiquitous clerestory roof, was extravagantly decorated in the rococo style of the period, plushly carpeted and well upholstered.

For night travel the upper berths were let down from their daytime position of being folded back against the upper walls of the car. The day seats were converted into comfortable lower berths. Thick curtains screened the sleeping quarters from the aisle, behind which, in order to preserve modesty, passengers performed all their preparations for the night.

Sleepers gradually became sectionalized and incorporated additional features for daytime comfort until by the 1920s, the most popular standard Pullman sleeping car had 12 sections and one drawing room with a sleeping capacity of 26 in upper and lower berths. A separate toilet cubicle and washrooms provided lounge chairs as well as toilet facilities. A rest room for women and a smoking room for men were situated at opposite ends of the car.

Below: Luxury long distance travel on the Canadian National Railways in the early 1930s: this car was paneled in English silver hardwood.

A somewhat belated swing towards greater privacy led to a complete rethink of Pullman sleeper design in the 1930s. They became 'all-room' cars offering a range of accommodation from roomettes with fold-down beds and self-contained toilet facilities, to bedrooms which, by folding back partitions, could be converted into a suite with drawing room.

Soon Pullman was leasing his unique cars, fully staffed and equipped by his own company, to railroads all over the country. But sleepers were only a beginning. Once the profit potential in providing a home-from-home for moneyed travelers was realized, resplendently luxurious parlor cars, diners and even complete private cars followed.

Pullman's pioneering on behalf of his fellow man's creature comforts – those who could afford them, at least – reached a widely welcomed highspot with the introduction of the first dining car, the *Delmonico*, in 1868. Before dining cars became essential features of long-distance trains, passengers had had to snatch hurried meals at restaurants during scheduled stops along the way. One magazine journalist, writing in 1873, complained that 'it was necessary to look at one's watch to tell whether it was breakfast, dinner or supper, these meals presenting invariably the same salient features of beefsteak, fried eggs, fried potato'.

Pullman not only provided first-class passengers

Left : A quick-lunch counter area in the lounge car of the New Orleans-Chicago Panama Limited of the Illinois Central Railroad in the 1950s.
Below : The Chuck Wagon car of the Burlington route's Denver Zephyr had this 19-seat coffee-shop at one end and an economy lunch counter at the other; both rooms were finished in an Old West decor of copper fixtures and saddle leather.

Below center : Spacious rest rooms on Santa Fe's new Hi-level El Capitan are located on the lower deck of each chair car.
Below bottom : The lounge car on the Super Chief of the Santa Fe Railroad.

with meals on the move at the appropriate times, but the cooking and service provided by his own chefs and waiters could compare favorably with that offered by the best restaurants. By 1874 there were more than 200 diners carried by long-distance trains throughout the USA and soon no express would consider leaving the terminal without at least one dining car. Pullman's early example was avidly followed and railroads were soon vying with each other to provide the best food at the best value.

Crack named trains, such as New York Central's Twentieth Century Limited, prided themselves on the epicurean heights which their à la carte menus scaled, while at the other end of the railway spectrum 'a dollar in the diner' throughout the heyday of passenger traffic, would buy a substantial and well-prepared meal.

The parlor car, which first made its appearance through the good offices of George Pullman around the time of his dining cars, served a dual purpose. Its fine appointments and fittings, comfortable easy chairs and refreshment service by Pullman waiter, provided a daytime diversion for long-distance travelers glad of a change from their sleeping quarters. It also provided accommodation for first-class 'way' travelers who had no need of a sleeping berth. Lounge and club cars are the direct modern descendants of the old parlor car.

Southern Pacific Railroad's flame-colored Daylight observation car is being loaded in San Francisco, 1952.
Inset : In the 1970s, Canadian Pacific Railroad built double-decker gallery-type passenger cars to attract the public.

The opportunities for elegant travel reached their height with private or hotel cars in which the rich could live, eat, entertain and sleep in self-indulgent luxury for the duration of the journey. Lavishly decorated and furnished, a private car would consist of dining rooms, saloons, bedrooms and kitchen.

A prestigious party would hire a whole train of private and sleeping cars, which might include a complete car divided into smoking rooms, a barber-shop and ice boxes in the baggage car. One delegation from the Chamber of Commerce of Cincinnati, which chartered a 'hotel train' for an early excursion to the west, reported that one car was arranged so that 'in the daytime it is an elegant saloon, fitted up with sofas on either side, leaving ample space for dancing. Built into the car is a fine parlor organ which, under the fingers of some passenger, furnishes the music for a cotillion . . .'

'The sleeping cars are fitted up with oiled walnut, carved and gilded, etched and stained plate glass, metal trappings heavily silver plated, seats cushioned with thick plushes, washstands of marble and walnut, damask curtains, and massive mirrors in frames of gilded walnut. The floors are carpeted with the most costly Brussels, and the roof beautifully frescoed in mosaics of gold, emerald, green, crimson, sky-blue, violet, drab and black.'

At this time passenger cars were the old familiar ornate all-wooden structures, but the number of accidents in which the insubstantial carriages either splintered and disintegrated or went up in flames, led at the beginning of the twentieth century first to massive steel underframes and then, a few years later, to all-steel construction. With the simultaneous growth of carriages to lengths of 85 feet or more, the weight of a single car could reach the 80 ton mark.

With this level of loading, a big train such as the Century which in the 1920s was regularly hauling 11 cars, would reach a total weight of more than 900 tons. The first reaction against this increasingly cumbersome rolling stock came in the 1930s when the Budd Company of Philadelphia developed a lightweight car constructed with sides of thin-gauge stainless steel, corrugated to give it load-bearing qualities. The traditional clerestory roof disappeared and the two six-wheel trucks, which had been needed to support the old heavyweight carriages, were reduced to two of four wheels. Although the Budd car was 85 feet long and carried additional equipment for the comfort of passengers, the overall weight was reduced to about 60 tons.

**Top left : This modern commuter car is run by the Pennsylvania Railroad.
Right : One of the Metroliner-style Amfleet coaches which forms the San Diegan Express that runs from Los Angeles to San Diego.**

Another traditional feature which was lost to progress during the early years of the twentieth century was the familiar open platform of the rear-end observation car – once an essential tail to any self-respecting passenger train. The brass-railed platforms gradually gave way to those enclosed with picture windows; this removed some of the hazards as well as some of the pleasures involved in allowing passengers to stand on this outside vantage point.

With the arrival of streamlining, observation cars followed suit with the large windows running the length of the carriage and around the bow-shaped rear end giving passengers the same wide-angle view of the passing scenery. After World War II, the dome car was introduced; it went one better than the observation car by providing a total vista – The California Zephyr of 1949, was one of the first trains with extensive application of this and travelers appreciated its windows all round and above, allowing an uninterrupted view of the surrounding country, which in the case of the CZ was certainly worth seeing. The dome car was added to many trains on western scenic routes – an area to which they are largely limited, in fact, because of the extra clearance needed for the dome.

Other developments followed; Santa Fe equipped its famous El Capitan with cars which carried passengers on the whole length of a top deck, while service requirements were catered for on a lower deck. Double-deck commuter cars were also supplied for a number of railroads.

The postwar period was also notable for the demise of Pullman. In 1947 an antitrust suit was brought against the company ordering it to cease either the manufacturing or the owning of its cars. Pullman decided to opt for the former and the cars

were sold to a consortium of the railroads on which they operated. Arrangements were made for Pullman to continue to run them, but even these ceased – after a century of operation – on 31 December 1968.

At its zenith in the 1920s, Pullman owned and ran 9860 Pullman cars and entertained 100,000 guests each night, 36 million in the course of the year. Every aspect of hospitality was covered in minute detail with instruction books and rules and, in

Above: Santa Fe's Hi-Level chair cars devoted the top level to seating and the lower level to baggage, rest-rooms, and services.

Below: The interior of a double-deck coach used for commuter traffic. The exterior of this train is pictured on page 136.

consequence, Pullman's reputation for service was a byword.

In the late 1970s, under Amtrak's patronage, carbuilders are again receiving substantial orders for main line passenger equipment. However, as yet there is little sign of anything new which might contribute to passengers' convenience.

The vagaries of time have had relatively little effect on standard American freight rolling stock. The century-old boxcar is still much in its original form except that steel construction has replaced wood and longer, heavier patterns have demanded bigger trucks. Flatcars which once carried rails to the ends of growing transcontinentals now, in enlarged form, play their integral role in the vast nation-wide piggyback operation. Modern industrial demands, of course, have resulted in adaptations and innovations. The traditional hopper is supplemented by vacuum and pressure unloading systems; there are refrigerated, temperature controlled and insulated boxcars; the removable roof of covered gondolas may consist of steel sections; stock cars run to two decks with adjustable louvers; three-deck auto transporters provide movement on a scale unknown in the rest of the world. Another type of transporter carries motor cars in pairs on end and so the variety goes on.

The most revolutionary and fast growing type of freight transport of recent years must be the piggyback system introduced in 1953. Southern Pacific was the first railroad to grasp the potential of a new Pullman-Standard 75-foot flat designed to carry truck trailers straight from the road, complete with load. SP quickly established a regular run in conjunction with its associated trucking operation, Pacific Motor Freight, between Los Angeles and San Francisco.

New York Central experimented with containers in the 1920s with some success, but fears on the part of the ICC that such a radical change would undermine their artificial rate structure led to insistence that NYC charge equally artificial high rates for container movement. In this way the ICC succeeded in holding back this development for a couple of decades.

The idea caught on in spectacular fashion and between 1955 and 1965 the number of wagonloads transported by piggyback grew from under 200,000 to over one million. Today's piggybacking flatcar carries either containers or trailers on its 87-foot loading deck. The wagons may be carried in mixed freight trains or comprise special fast all-piggyback freights with a loading of around 2000 tons. Related

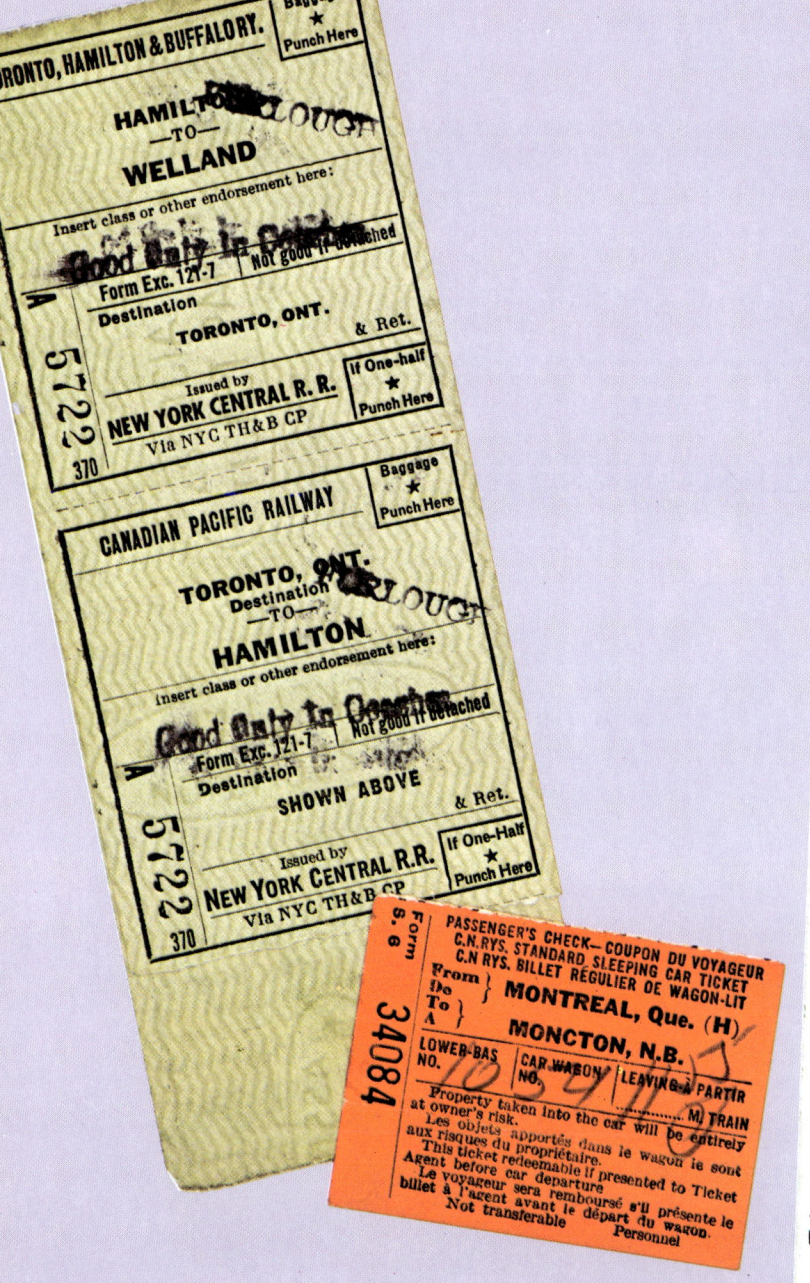

to the piggyback operation is the carriage of containers, mostly built to International Standards Organization standards and since these circulate in and between many of the countries of the world by ship, the railroads became part of a worldwide transport network.

One component of a freight train has existed unchanged – at least in spirit – since the early days of long-distance railroading; this is the caboose. The rear car of a freight train provides a home from home for the crew today in exactly the same way it did a century ago. One old western railroader, describing his train's caboose around the 1880s, eulogized: 'We had a fine, big, eight-wheeled caboose, right out of the paint shop, red outside and green inside. There were six bunks in her, a row of lockers on each side to sit on and keep supplies in, a stove and table, and a desk for the conductor. We furnished our own bedding and cooking utensils, and we had a pleasant and comfortable home on wheels. As the boys had good taste, we soon had the car looking like a young lady's boudoir. We had lace curtains in front of the bunks, a mat the flagman had swiped from a sleeping car, a dog and a canary.' The same spirit no doubt prevails in the caboose of today – though the lace cur-

Top: Ancient Caboose –
four wheeled vehicles
were always rare but are
now extinct on the rail-
roads of North America.
Above: Modern 'Caboose'
this one belongs to the
Chicago, Milwaukee, St
Paul & Pacific Railroad
and is very different to
the one above.

tains might not find such a ready reception, any more than radio communication with the cab, up to a mile away, would have had with the old railroader of un-usually refined taste. The tragedy, of course is that there ought not to be a caboose and a rear-end crew. Only one railroad has dared challenge the unions on this issue – Florida East Coast. On FEC the conductor rides in the cab with the engineer; there is plenty of room since FEC do not employ firemen on their fireless locomotives. The caboose is in fact replaced by a small automatic radio transmitter attached to the coupler of the rear car of the train.

Amongst North America's two million plus freight cars there is not only great variety in design but also great variety of ownership. Apart from the railroads, a large number of other companies, specialist car-owners as well as normal industrial enterprises, own fleets of cars. Each owner, mindful of his ownership of a high, wide and handsome mobile bill-board, sees that his vehicles are painted in vivid colors with his name, his herald and his slogan clearly written upon them.

Any car that leaves its parent road – *interchange* is the term used – must meet quite stringent require-ments in addition to the usual safety regulations laid down by the ICC. Cars more than 50 years old are not accepted for interchange, for example. Once interchange has taken place, the car owner is entitled to his *per diem*, which is a fixed daily rental. Moreover, the railroad on which the car is running is not only liable for its repair if it breaks down but is also liable for any damage it might do because of its faulty condition. All in all, interchange is a dubious business and railroads, like those in Canada for example, which carry a high proportion of their traffic within their own system, are very lucky.

All that remains to be said is that the North American car fleet, with all the arrangements for universal circulation over the length and breadth of Canada, the USA and Mexico, is an asset of enormous value. In hard cash terms its replacement cost, at a conservative $25,000 per unit, would be 50 billion dollars.

Below: A highway trailer is lifted off a flatcar in Luther yard in St Louis, Missouri. This system, called 'piggybacking' is used for shipping goods across oceans as well as continents.

Top: A hopper car is covered to protect goods which might be affected by weather.
Right: The eternal box-car! Note the herald and slogan on the top half; the dimensions and weights below.

GREAT TRAINS NOW NO MORE

No named train epitomizes the lost glory of American railways better than New York Central's Twentieth Century Limited. It became so celebrated it was a national symbol, a byword for prestige and luxury. There was no shortage of well-heeled passengers waiting to walk the red carpet rolled out specially for Century travelers. Profits from the premium fares were excellent and its eventual demise was the result of railroad miscalculation on a grandiose scale. The Century became a microcosm of railway malaise.

From its inception on 15 June 1902, the Twentieth Century Limited – both the train and its title – caught the mood of the moment. By 1926 the NYC could refer to it, without any fear of dissent, as 'A National Institution'. Visitors were told that they had not seen America unless they had 'ridden the Century', and its image of up-to-the-minute luxury travel lasted for more than 60 years. Yet eight years later it was no longer in use.

The service was introduced by the New York Central & Hudson River Railroad and the Lake Shore

Left : The City of Los Angeles traverses the Nevada Canyons on the approach to Las Vegas. Below : In early days the Twentieth Century Limited was made up of wooden cars and hauled by an Atlantic. Preceding spread : The Santa Fe all-Pullman Super Chief climbs Cajon Pass in California behind four diesel-electric units on its daily run to Chicago in the 1950s.

& Michigan Southern Railroad (who later merged as the NYC) over their joint 961 mile route between New York and Chicago. The 'Water Level Route', as Central's slogan had it, was a longer but smoother ride than the rival Pennsylvania Special's 908 mile course over the Allegheny mountains and it cut four hours, then later six and finally eight, off the 24-hour standard for the run.

From the start the accent was on speed and comfort with an all-Pullman train. From three sleepers, a diner and a combined library-buffet car on its maiden trips, it soon grew to include a combination club car, two diners, a ten-compartment sleeping car, two sleeping cars with seven compartments and two drawing rooms, four sleeping cars each with twelve sections, a compartment and a drawing room, and one sleeper with twelve sections and a drawing room. Such was its popularity in the golden years, that the train was often run in sections – up to eight at times – with two diners in each section.

Massive all-steel equipment had replaced the original wooden cars between 1910 and 1912 and it may be noted that the services offered included: barber, both fresh and salt-water baths, valet, ladies' maid, manicure, stenographer and telephone service while standing in terminals. Two other things were significant; part of the extra-fare supplement was refunded to passengers if the train was late and, furthermore, a note of the train's performance, distinguished passengers on board and so on, was placed on the NYC President's desk each morning.

With the introduction of streamlining and so-called lightweight stock in 1938, the Century became an all-room train, with small 'roomettes' bigger bedrooms, drawing rooms, compartments, and ultra-luxurious suites consisting of drawing room, bedroom and shower. By the 1950s a nine-car Century could carry 200 passengers with accommodation consisting of 30 roomettes with fold-down bed and toilet, 79 double bedrooms, four drawing rooms, four compartments, a club lounge, diners, a baggage car and post office car at the head and bringing up the rear, an observation lounge.

But by then the end was near; the knell had been sounded more than 20 years before when a promo-

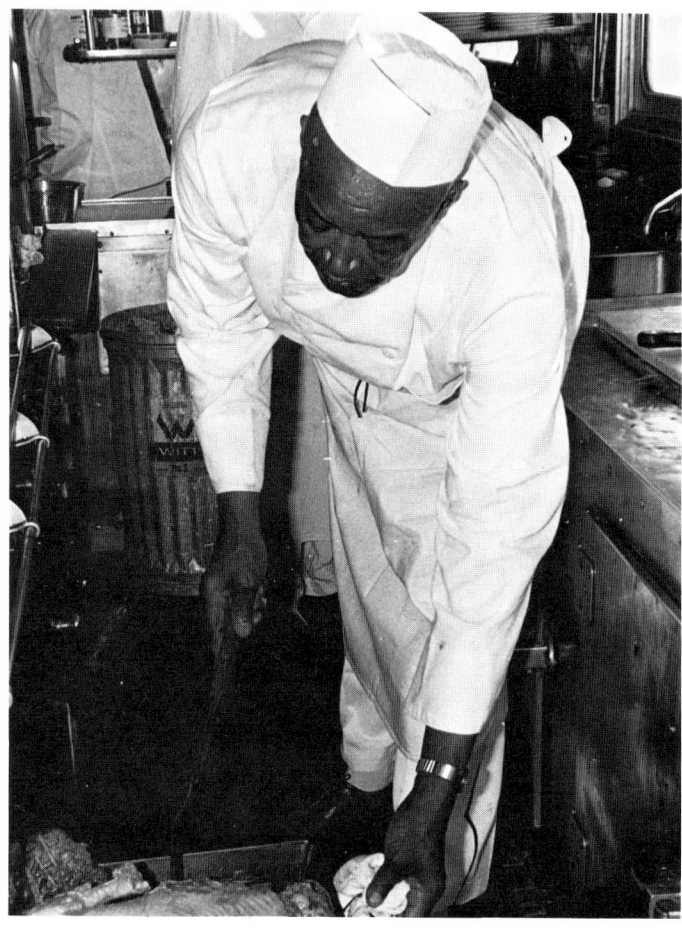

Above : A chef working at his oven in the kitchen of a Southern Pacific dining car.
Right : The observation lounge, *Hickory Creek,* of the Twentieth Century Limited.

tional booklet about the train stated unequivocally: 'If it were not financially successful the merest novice would know that it could not long continue to run – at least, not in its present high fashion.'

For many years it was extraordinarily successful; so much so that it played a large part making the New York–Chicago line the most passenger-oriented of all the major lines in the US. By the beginning of World War II the Century had grossed $150 million, but after 1945 passenger traffic never reverted to prewar levels. New York Central had one last go at re-equipping the Century, this time to the tune of nearly $4 million. Innovations included diesel traction, fluorescent lighting throughout and pneumatically operated doors.

The Century first felt the cold wind of change in April 1958 when the train's all-Pullman tradition came to an end with the introduction of sleeper coaches and reclining seat cars at second-class prices. The move, however, did nothing to improve the revenue situation and though the Century struggled on through the merger of a now sick New York Central with an ailing Pennsylvania Railroad, its reprieve was short-lived. The Twentieth Century Limited made its last run in 1970, the same catastrophic year Penn Central went bankrupt.

Second place in the Limiteds' hall of fame is Santa Fe's Super Chief which made history in its own particular way. The exquisitely appointed train was the first diesel-powered all-Pullman streamliner in the US when it was introduced in 1937 and it complemented the luxury with a running time of 39.5 hours from Chicago to Los Angeles, a cut of over 15 hours from that of its predecessor, the famous Chief.

The Super had an excellent pedigree, coming from – and preceding – a long line of passenger trains

Left : A full-length diner on New York Central's Twentieth Century Limited.
Top : The Twentieth Century Limited speeds along the Hudson River.

which were considered for many years to be among the best in the country. The first Chief – advertised as 'Extra fast, extra fine and extra fare' – was introduced in 1926 following two earlier luxury trains – the California Limited and the Santa Fe De Luxe.

Though the Santa Fe gained 12 times the revenue from freight as from its passenger services, the company was renowned for the service it gave to its passengers. Superb food was a speciality and a ride on this train was an experience. Economy measures after 1960 involved the operational – but not commercial – combination of the Super Chief with the all-coach El Capitan. They still occupied separate columns in the 'timetable', but the times shown were identical. Of course, each train had its own facilities.

Santa Fe, being a prosperous and efficient railroad and mindful of its reputation, never offered a lower quality of service on the Super Chief (or El Capitan for that matter) in spite of mounting losses and, when Amtrak took over in 1970, matters continued as before. However, Santa Fe entered the *caveat* that the name was only to be used as long as, in its opinion, proper service continued to be offered. In due time Amtrak, in leveling up the standard of most of the nation's passenger trains, had to level down that of the Super Chief. In 1973, therefore, the railroad stood on its rights and Amtrak's Chicago – Los Angeles train is now called the South-West Limited.

Another Chicago – Los Angeles route was run by Union Pacific via Omaha. The diesel-hauled 11-car City of Los Angeles jointly owned with Chicago & North-Western Railway, started offering weekly service in May 1936; demand was such that an order for a new 17-car train was placed almost immediately. By 1941 delivery of further equipment meant that

every-third-day service could be offered. After a wartime interval when streamliners were not appropriate, sufficient new equipment was available – in UP's handsome golden yellow and scarlet colors – to provide daily service. Three streamliners used the Overland route called the Cities of Los Angeles, Portland and San Francisco, each serving the city of its name. By 1955, the trains were being routed from Omaha to Chicago over the Milwaukee Railroad instead of C & NW and had dome dining cars for 'roof garden' eating on the move. By 1969, the Overland train still ran, but retrenchment meant just one combined 'City of Everything' out of Chicago. Amtrak never continued even this remnant of the City of Los Angeles.

In Chapter 7, mention was made of the Chicago, Burlington and Quincy Railroad and the early diesel streamliners developed for it. By 1936 the rapidly growing fleet included the Denver Zephyr 12-car trains with diner, sleepers and observation car. By the beginning of World War II many Zephyrs ran on the Burlington routes and in 1947 they became the first trains to include the now-familiar Vistadome cars in their formation. By the time the famous California Zephyr appeared in 1949 it carried up to five dome cars for its 2525-mile run over the Burlington, Denver and Rio Grande Western and Western Pacific railroads.

The California Zephyr was a pioneer, in that, unlike most named trains which then tried to combine speed and luxury, its speed as an ingredient was replaced by the scenic splendor of the route. The CZ's schedule was deliberately arranged so that the most spectacular sections of the route were traversed in daylight. With a route that took in the Moffat tunnel, the Rockies, traversed Utah and Nevada, and passed through the Feather River canyon, it was easy to see why speed took second place.

With such a memorable route, CZ was never short of passengers. Rising costs took their toll, nevertheless, and the train ceased to run in 1970. Amtrak's Chicago to Oakland train called the San Francisco Zephyr (it never reaches the city of its name) bears no resemblance in route and little in service to the old California Zephyr. Rio Grande, outside Amtrak, runs a daytime mini-CZ (called the Rio Grande Zephyr) over its segment of the original route from Denver to Salt Lake City.

Rio Grande until 1951 ran the San Juan. It was a short-distance train and traveled slowly and its considerable fame has not been dimmed by a lapse of 25 years. The San Juan was a narrow-gauge train which provided a daily coach, parlor, buffet, mail, express and observation car service over 200 scenic miles from Alamosa to Durango, Colorado. Its maximum speed was 35 mph and it was powered by steam to the end.

The Norfolk and Western's Pocahontas, was also powered by steam and ran from Norfolk to Cincinatti, in the daytime, taking the same overall time as the San Juan, but covering two-and-a-half times the distance.

However the queen of America's daytime trains was undoubtedly Southern Pacific's Daylight service, along the coastal route between Los Angeles and San Francisco. Special orange and silver streamlined coaches and cars were built for this train in 1938 with, in addition, some rather beautiful matching 4-8-4 steam locomotives. Superb decor, a fast timing (30 minutes less than the substitute train Coast Starlight which does the run today) and excellent service gave the Daylights a sky-high reputation.

One could list great trains and great names of the past forever . . . Capitol Limited, Overland Limited, Orange Blossom Special, Forty-Niner, Merchants Limited, New England States and so on. There were some lesser great names, like Flying Crow, for example, among the 400-plus North American train names no longer on the timetables, referred to in Arthur D Dubin's two definitive volumes on the subject *Some Classic Trains* and *More Classic Trains*; but in general the names are evocative, descriptive and worthy of the great trains they dignified and which have now gone forever.

Left : The magnificent steam train, the Coast Daylight, was not replaced by a diesel until 1955.
Right : The 1937 Super Chief running between Chicago and Los Angeles was the USA's first all-Pullman diesel-powered streamliner, making two 2227-mile round trips weekly.
Below : The DRGW's narrow-gauge San Juan Express near Sublette, Colorado in 1949, two years before withdrawal. The engine is *Sports Model* 2-8-2 No 476.

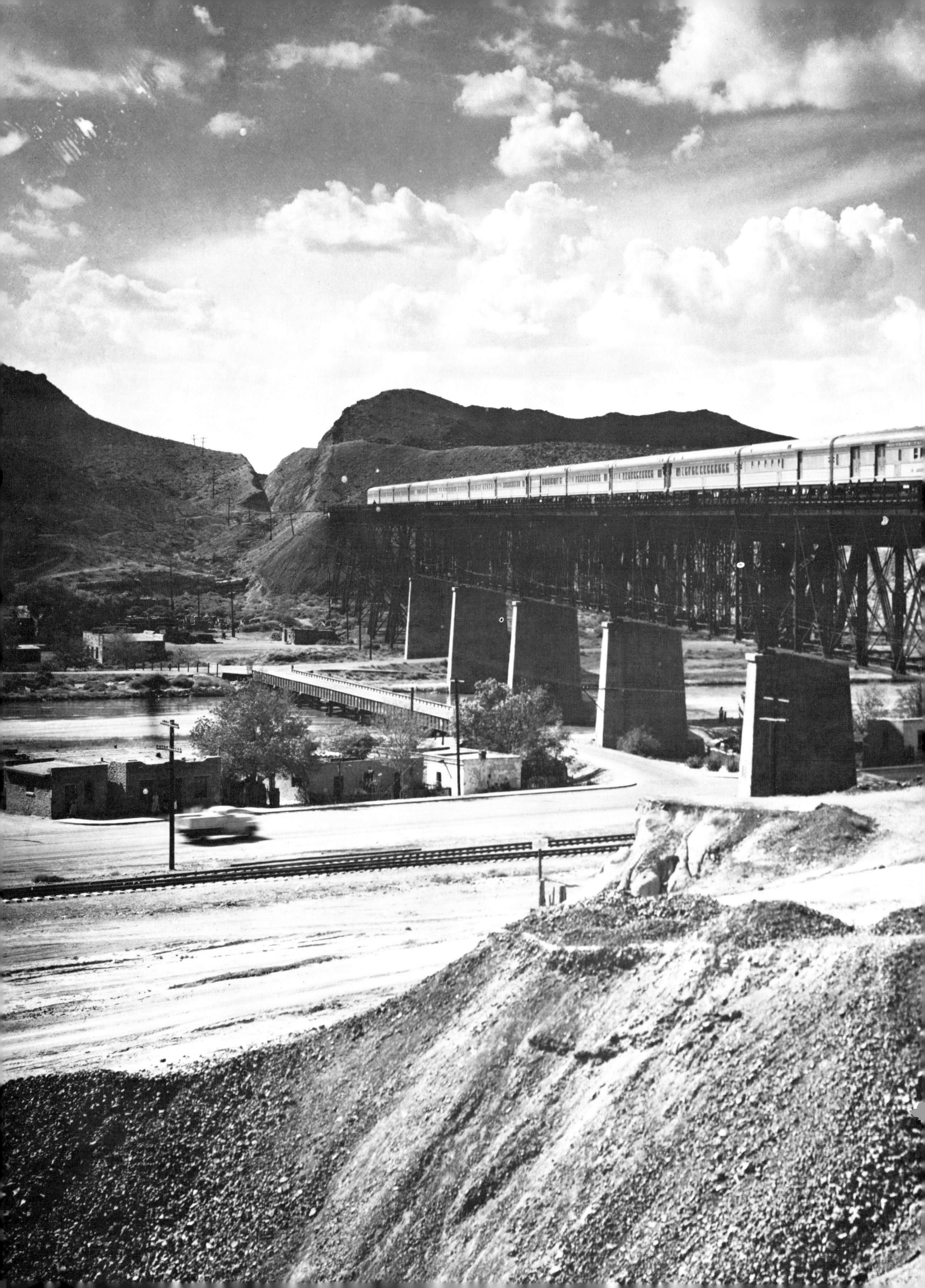

GREAT TRAINS
WITH US STILL

GREAT TRAINS WITH US STILL

Almost all the main line passenger trains running in the USA at the end of 1970 had to clear the hurdle of Amtrak's remit to provide service only on certain selected routes. About half of these trains did survive and these are the ones that are with us still, although with different names and routes in many cases. Whether they are still great must be left to the reader to judge, but what stands out is that they are not the same as they used to be.

Pullman, who for so long provided everything on most lines with more comfort than the basic coach seat, left a tradition of good service that has helped in building the new era. This service was no accident; every eventuality, frequent or infrequent, was provided for in a thick manual of instructions. There

Left : Castle Crags near Dunsmuir provide some of the spectacular scenery along the Portland-San Francisco route of Southern Pacific's summertime streamliner, the *Shasta Daylight*.
Below : Northern Pacific's No 3, *The Alaskan*, 'doubleheads' out of Missoula, Montana ready for the heavy climb west.
Preceding spread : The New Orleans-San Francisco Sunset Limited of the Southern Pacific sported a livery of stainless steel and orange, west of El Paso, Texas.

were only two ways of solving a problem – the Pullman way or the Wrong way. Take, for example, a simple request from a client for a glass of beer. . . .

Beer

1. Ascertain from passenger what kind of Beer is desired.

2. Arrange set-up on bar tray in buffet: one cold bottle of Beer, which has been wiped, standing upright: glass (No 11) 2/3 full of finely chopped ice (for chilling purpose – making it a distinctive service); glass (No 12); bottle opener; and paper cocktail napkin. Attendant should carry a clean glass towel on his arm with fold pointing toward his hand while rendering service.

3. Proceed to passenger with above set-up.

4. Place bar tray with set-up on table (or etc).

5. Place paper cocktail napkin on table in front of passenger.

6. Present bottle of Beer to passenger displaying label and cap. Return bottle to bar tray.

7. Pour ice from chilled glass (No 11) into glass (No 12).

8. Open bottle of Beer with bottle opener in presence of passenger (holding bottle at an angle), pointing neck of bottle away from passenger; wipe top of bottle with clean glass towel.

9. Pour Beer into glass (No 11) by placing top of bottle into glass, and slide the beer down the side until beer reaches about 2 inches from top – then put a collar on the beer by dropping a little in the glass which now should be upright.

10. Place glass containing Beer on paper cocktail napkin.

11. Place bottle containing remainder of Beer on table before passenger, with label facing him.

12. Remove bar tray with equipment not needed by passenger and return to the buffet.

Left : This ranch car of Great Northern Railway's Empire Builder had a coffee shop and lounge featuring pinto leather, livestock brands, branding irons, paneled sides, beams and a mural.

Above : One of the earliest American light-weight diesel stream-liners, the three-car articulated 600-hp Flying Yankee of the Boston & Maine Central was built in 1935.

beautiful and very comfortable, being complete with dome cars and all the usual facilities.

One always speaks of a train like this in the singular, but in reality this is not true. For example in this particular case, at 12 noon, Canadian No 1 is rolling between Montreal and Ottawa, No 2 is by Lake Superior's north shore, No 3 is approaching Calgary from the east, No 4 is in the yards at Vancouver being serviced in readiness for a 1715 departure, No 5 is eastbound through the most superb scenery of the run – at Lake Louise in the Rockies, No 6 is crossing the prairies east of Winnipeg, No 7 is at North Bay between Sudbury and Ottawa with the expectation of reaching Montreal by 2030 and so becoming No 1 again. To equip the Canadian and re-equip the Dominion to run as a second section, CP had to order 173 cars. At present only one service runs, but with more carriages when necessary.

At the same time, Canadian National, the second of the two transcontinental railroads with its longer route, has eight Super-Continentals in action simultaneously, not to speak of general passenger service over one-third of its 25,000 mile network, including seven other sleeping and dining car train services.

Left: The Canadian, enters the spiral tunnel on the ascent of the Kicking Horse Pass. At any one time in Canada there are at least six more of these trains carrying passengers across the continent.

Below: Amtrak's frequent high-speed Metroliner service on the northeast corridor of the New York to Washington route enters Philadelphia's 30th Street Station.

Amtrak's idea of good service is perhaps more suitable to these egalitarian days; the client is handed his can of beer and plastic 'glass' over the bar counter; he then opens and pours it out and, when finished, puts the can himself in a trash bag thoughtfully placed, open, in a corner of the lounge car.

Amtrak is able to offer two advantages; first, routings by the most convenient means regardless of ownership and also the boon of an all-line unlimited travel USA-railpass for 14, 21 or 30 days. Amtrak has also re-introduced through, coast-to-coast sleeping cars, which, in the absence of a true transcontinental railroad, have until now presented problems.

First, however, we must look at the North American country which has not one but two transcontinental trains; both have changed little from their inception and are also in the hands of the same owners who introduced them. The first is the Canadian, which was a new train put into service in 1954, to supplant the old Dominion. Canadian Pacific had the advantage of experience gained with new postwar trains in the USA and, accordingly, the red and stainless steel streamliner was both very

Amtrak has 50 named trains on its timetable, the majority of which are famous. Most distinguished is the Broadway Limited which makes the run from New York (and Washington) to Chicago and vice versa every night. This is one of the only two through trains to Chicago from New York. Incidentally, as recently as 1956 there were eight other daily trains between these cities on the Pennsylvania Railroad alone and a further dozen or so by other routes. The Broadway Limited is younger than its rival the Twentieth Century, the first Broadway Limited leaving either terminus on 24 November 1912. It was an existing de luxe train, called the Pennsylvania Special which was re-named to avoid confusion with the Pennsylvania Limited. The Broadway took a holiday during World War I, but came back after-

Above left : The success of the City of Portland prompted Union Pacific to order four more streamlined expresses. This 17-car City of Los Angeles, jointly owned by Union Pacific and Chicago & North Western Railroads, was inaugurated on the run between Chicago and the west coast in December 1937.
Left : The North Coast Limited emerges from Nimrod Tunnel as it races through Hell Gate Canyon.

Right : The City of Los Angeles, a streamlined train with several dome cars, winds its way through the hills of Weber Canyon, near Ogden, Utah in 1962. Below left : Amtrak's modern streamlined Panama Limited takes on passengers and goods at a station on its Chicago-New Orleans run. It is headed by new General Electric P-30 diesels.

wards. The amenities were similar to those of the Century and, again similarly, it was re-equipped as a streamliner in 1938 and again after the war. Unlike the Century, however, the Pennsy's train remained all-sleeper, apparently because the quality of the service offered had just that edge over Central's. In 1964 Arthur Dubin described a typical train west-bound at Pittsburg – which implied no lack of patronage – as follows . . .

3-unit diesel – sleepers, *Chippewa Creek, Clear Creek, Imperial Lea, Illinois Rapids, Alfred E Hunt* – diners 4622 and 4623 – sleepers *Imperial Fields, Miami Rapids, Charles Lockhart, Fishing Rapids, Clearfield Rapids* – sleeper-bar-lounge-observation *Tower View.*

Between New York and Harrisburg a single GG1 electric locomotive would have done the work of the three diesels. By this time the Century had been downgraded to a sleeper-coach train for six years. The Broadway survived the PRR's merger with NYC, as well as the subsequent bankruptcy, to run in Amtrak's hands, although it now includes coaches, as well as sleepers.

Amtrak had a problem with its service from Chicago to the northwest. Three famous trains, the

Empire Builder, North Coast Limited and Olympian Hiawatha (originally Great Northern, Northern Pacific and Chicago, Milwaukee St Paul & Pacific respectively) were to be reduced to two. It was neatly solved by retaining the Empire Builder and calling the other the North Coast Hiawatha.

Actually, the North Coast Limited should have had pride of place. It was introduced on 29 April 1900 to run from St Paul to Seattle, but in 1911 it started back from Chicago. Following the general pattern, the train became a streamliner in 1947 and a dome-liner in 1954 and it is this route which Amtrak's train follows.

The rival Empire Builder dates from 1929; its name is that by which the dynamic Canadian founder of the GN, James J Hill, was known. Its introduction

Top : GNR's streamlined Empire Builder is building up speed across the plains near Fort Browning, Montana for its haul over the Great Divide.

Right : Here the Empire Builder is roaring through the Rockies with the scenic Mount St Nicholas in the background.

159

Right: One of the latest solutions to the passenger problem is this turbo-train which runs on Canadian National lines between Toronto and Montreal. Note the similarity between this train and the M-10001 pictured on page 106.
Bottom: The Freedom Train, resurrected by Southern Pacific, is pulled by 4-8-4 No 4449 in Mendota, Illinois in 1975.
Far right: The Mount Washington Cog Railway.

coincided with the opening of the electrified 7.75 mile Cascade Tunnel. Streamlining came in 1947, with a further re-equipment in 1951 and finally domes arrived in 1955.

The Olympian Hiawatha (and, indeed, all the other Hiawatha trains) should more correctly belong in the previous chapter, but readers will have noted the attention given to these remarkable creations in the accounts of both steam and electric traction. The Olympian Hiawatha ran for over 650 miles under the wires, more than any other American train, and it is good that an echo of its name survives in the area – if not the exact route – on which it ran. The train arrived in 1947, a streamliner to replace the Olympian which dated from the line's opening in 1909. Competition kept those who offered service on these three great trains on their toes and it is to be hoped that Amtrak, without this spur, can maintain standards on the two it runs.

Similar competitive conditions made for an even more complex picture when travel to Florida is considered. Complications occur because successive sections of the route were in the hands of different railroads, with the possibility of endless permutations and combinations. No attempt can be made here to unravel these, but perhaps we might look at the trains presently offered and then glance at their origins.

Autotrain has already been mentioned; this bit of profitable private enterprise railroading takes the passenger's automobile in the baggage car and offers service from both Washington and St Louis. Amtrak has three trains, Silver Meteor, Silver Star and Champion from New York and Washington and The Floridian from Chicago. The last named is the newest, dating only from Amtrak days and is the only one of the four to include a dome car. The others date back to the new streamliners introduced in 1939 by various railroads, principally Seaboard Air Line, Atlantic Coast line and Florida East Coast Railroad. Some wonderful names, like Orange Blossom Special, have gone but today's relatively lavish provision of trains makes for a good future for rail transport in this world-famous vacation state.

Continuing on this optimistic note there is a famous train whose facilities have much improved in recent years. This is Southern Pacific's Sunset Limited which runs from New Orleans to Los Angeles. It has the longest history of any train mentioned in this chapter, having been introduced as a solid weekly all-Pullman train in 1894. Lucius Beebe wrote in *The Trains We Rode* . . . 'the concept of a grand hotel was everywhere visible on the Espee in the form of watermarked stationary, silver finger-bowls, an encouraging assortment of fine whiskeys on the club cars, out-of-season strawberries, Eastern lobster and fresh brook trout on the menu and conductors who were very much the Viceroys in an Imperial scheme of things from Management at

NOON POSITION

All Passenger Trains with diner and/or sleeping car that are timed to be en route at noon on a Friday in the Winter 1976/7 timetable are shown; AMTRAK unless otherwise specified.

Key to Railroads BLACK

ACR Alagoma Central Railway
AM Amtrak (North-East Corridor)
AT & SF Atchison, Topeka & Santa Fe
BN Burlington Northern
CN Canadian National
CON Conrail
CP Canadian Pacific
D & RGW Denver & Rio Grande Western
IC Illinois Central
L & N Louisville & Nashville
MP Missouri Pacific
N & W Norfolk & Western
QNS & L Quebec North Shore & Labrador
SCL Seaboard Coast Line
SOU Southern Railway
SP Southern Pacific

Key to Trains BLUE

A ADIRONDACK *New York – Montreal*
C CANADIAN (CP) *Montreal – Vancouver*
Ch CHAMPION *New York – St. Petersburg*
CS COAST STARLIGHT *Los Angeles – Seattle*
EB EMPIRE BUILDER *Chicago – Seattle*
F FLORIDIAN *Chicago – Miami*
IA INTER AMERICAN *Chicago – Laredo*
JWR JAMES WHITCOMB RILEY *Chicago – Cincinnati*
LS LONE STAR *Chicago – Houston*
LSL LAKE SHORE LIMITED *New York – Chicago*
M MOUNTAINEER *Chicago – Norfolk*
NC NORTH COAST HIAWATHA *Chicago – Seattle*
NR NIAGARA RAINBOW *New York – Detroit*
O OCEAN (CN) *Montreal – Halifax*
P PANAMA LIMITED *Chicago – New Orleans*
RGZ RIO GRANDE ZEPHYR (D & RGW) *Denver – Salt Lake City*
S SCOTIAN (CN) *Montreal – Halifax*
SC SUPER CONTINENTAL (SC) *Montreal – Vancouver*
SFZ SAN FRANCISCO ZEPHYR *Chicago – Oakland*
SL SUNSET LIMITED *Los Angeles – New Orleans*
SM SILVER METEOR *New York – Miami*
SWL SOUTH WEST LIMITED *Chicago – Los Angeles*
SS SILVER STAR *New York – Miami*
ST SOUTHERN CRESCENT (SR) *Washington – New Orleans*
1 Sault Ste. Marie to Hearst (ACR)
2 Sept Iles to Schefferville (QNS & L)
9 Edmonton to Prince Rupert (CN)
93/94 Winnipeg and Churchill (CN)
175 Quebec to Cochrane (CN)

Schefferville

QNS & L

2

Sept Iles

Hearst

Cochrane 175 CN Quebec

Si

CN

Oi Oii

Halifax

St. John's

SC vi ACR

SCi

CP

Sault Ste Marie 1

Cvi

Sii

Montreal

Ci

Aii

Toronto

NRi

Bi

LSLiii

New York

LSL i

NRii

CON

CON

NLiii

SSi

AM

JWR / M ii

Washington

Fi

Cincinnati CON

JWR

N & W

SSiii

Mi

Norfolk

L & N

SOU

SCL

STi

Birmingham

STii

Jacksonville

Chi

Chii

SSii Fii

SMii

SMi

Miami

0 100 200 300 400 500 m

The 2-4-4-T No 7 performs at Edaville for her fans on this, the first of all the pleasure lines.

1 Market Street, San Francisco downwards.' He adds 'The Sunset itself, taken in its finest hour, might well be the paradigm of all transcontinental luxury runs . . .' A new streamlined extra-fare Sunset went into service in 1950, but by 1970 it had lost both sleepers and diner, an automat buffet being the only facility available on this 44-hour run. Beebe, sadly for us – but perhaps fortunately for him – never lived to see it. Amtrak, one is delighted to find, soon restored not only sleepers and diner but also uses the train as a link in a transcontinental route between Los Angeles and New York, with through sleepers, which travelers can use as a hotel during an overnight stopover to enjoy the pleasures of New Orleans.

One type of train is still going from strength to strength. Pleasure trains are not new: more than 20 years before Horatio Allen gingerly set *Stourbridge Lion* in motion, a man called Richard Trevithick gave rides with a steam locomotive called *Catch-me-who-can* on a circular track in London, England. What is new in North America and unheard of for many years are passenger railroads with a high growth rate. The current 'Steam Passenger Service Directory' (PO Box 666, Middletown, NY 10940), which includes railroads worked by other forms of power and also static museums, has 126 entries. Ten years ago it had 80 and had it existed 30 years ago there would have been less than 12.

1947 was in fact the year when the new railroad age began. A man called Ellis D Attwood had acquired some quaint and charming narrow-gauge rolling stock from the defunct 24-inch gauge railways in the state of Maine, described in Chapter 6. He used them to make a 4.5-mile circular railroad on his cranberry farm and soon, just to help with

Top: In 1964, this 4-6-4 No 5632, preserved by the Chicago, Burlington & Quincy Railroad served as the Illini Railroad Club Special. Since that time it has retired from active life.

Above center: Southern Railway's preserved 2-8-2 thrills its fans at Manassas, Virginia, May 1976. Above: Another preserved 2-8-2 is ready to run on a pleasure railroad.

expenses, invited the public to take rides. 30 years later, the Edaville Railroad and transport museum (at South Carver, Massachusetts) is a major tourist attraction.

Edaville was a new creation; other cases arose where an abandoned railroad was taken over by amateurs with the intention of running it as a live museum. The little Strasburg Railroad in Pennsylvania was one of these. It was constructed way back in the 1830s and until 1953 had pursued a useful but uneventful career by connecting Strasburg with the Pennsylvania RR's main line at Paradise, east of Harrisburg. In that year the two-mile line faced abandonment but some far-sighted enthusiasts thought of running it as a live museum, using steam traction and vintage cars. This bold pioneering enterprise succeeded – the promoters even got their money back – and, like Edaville, Strasburg has gone on from strength to strength. This time the gauge was standard and, while this makes for bigger and therefore more costly parts and materials, the variety of exhibits could be greater with (in the case of steam locomotives) 40,000 to choose from instead of a mere handful. Strasburg is the only place in the east at which either a 'camel-back' or an 'American standard' can be seen running.

This is the classic type of preserved railroad; of course they can be standard-gauge like Strasburg or, like another in Pennsylvania, the East Broad Top, narrow-gauge. The EBT was a 36-inch gauge coal-hauling line which was sold as junk during the 1950s.

Below : A very old but well-preserved steam engine chugs along on a pleasure railroad in Muskoka, a very picturesque part of northern Ontario.
Bottom : The Green Mountain Railroad in Vermont uses an ex-Canadian Pacific 4-6-2 to pull its tourist train.

On Knott's Berry Farm
near Los Angeles, pas-
sengers can ride on an
ex-Denver & Rio Grande
Western narrow-gauge
2-8-0 which has been com-
pletely refurbished and
redecorated.

However, the scrap man had a soul and, unable to bear cutting up such a lovely thing, stayed his hand. In the end he kept the best five out of the 33 miles, including the headquarters and shops at Orbisonia and four of the elegant matching Baldwin 2-8-2s. Today the EBT is healthy and doing well hauling tourists, mainly because of the restraint shown in keeping the mileage and, hence, the number of rails,

spikes and ties to look after at a modest level. Long railroads that rely solely on tourism find the financial going rough.

Also in this category but very different are a dozen or so abandoned logging railroads which have been re-incarnated as tourist lines. Foremost here is the Cass Scenic Railroad in West Virginia; the climb to Bath Knob Mountain behind one of Cass' Shays is an exciting experience to which switchbacks and grades as steep as 14 percent contribute.

Next we come to the lines which have quite involuntarily become pleasure railroads. Preservation just crept up on them; when they realized what was happening, it was too late. One minute people used them for transportation, the next (or so it must have seemed) the customers were just out to enjoy the ride. The most notable example – now a national monument to be mentioned in the same breath as Niagara or the Grand Canyon – is the Silverton Train.

The Denver & Rio Grande Railroad in 1888 extended its narrow-gauge main line up the Canyon of the Lost Souls to the town of Silverton, which, as its name implies, was then the booming center of a

Left: Union Pacific Railroad's preserved 4-8-4 No 8444 makes a run past for photographers and 'train watchers' on the Denver-Cheyenne route. Left below: The 4-6-0 No 85 of the Oahu Railway in the Hawaiian Islands. Right: Sierra Railroad's 2-8-0 No 28 en route between Jamestown and Standard California.

mining area. By 1949 two short, mixed trains each week were sufficient to handle traffic, but rail-fans and tourists began to ride the ancient combine in increasing numbers. Ten years later, both freight and local passengers had vanished, but the tourists came in sufficient numbers to justify in summer a daily train using as many vintage cars as could be collected and an original genuine narrow-gauge Rio Grande 2-8-2. Later, some new steel cars were built and old fashioned open observation cars converted from standard-gauge open gondolas. By the late 1960s, two long daily trains were needed in season and, in spite of that, customers have to be turned away.

The ride up the Cañon de los Animas Perditas is exceedingly spectacular; at one point the little train crawls with squealing flanges along a narrow ledge 400 feet above the river. At other places it runs close (too close sometimes) to the tumbling water. There is something to travel for, also, because the inhabitants of Silverton help by putting on such attractions as a gun-fight, so realistic that on occasions participants have actually been hurt.

The next sort of pleasure railway is one which is genuinely new in all respects, not like Edaville which uses new track and old trains. There is no

Above: This Denver & Rio Grande Western Silverton train K-28 Sports Model 2-8-2 has been totally refurbished to perform in a movie.

Below: This 4-6-0 pulls a train through the Puget Sound and Snoqualmie Valley in Washington. On the right of this picture in the shed is a rotary snowplow of days gone by.

Amtrak's San Diegan leaves Los Angeles. Inset : Amtrak's Coast Starlight arrives at Los Angeles.

doubt which should be put forward as the premier line in this category. Walt Disney was a great rail fan – one has only to see his cartoon train *Casey Junior* to realize this – and when he created Disneyland he did so inside a brand new circular track on which real three-fifths full-size steam trains run. The only criticism is that the Santa Fe & Disneyland Railroad is a bit too perfect, clean and tidy. Real railroads are never like that. Two equally perfect 'American Standard' replica 4-4-0s were built in the Walt Disney shops for the opening; since then two more locomotives have been constructed using the basic shells of long set-aside plantation engines. The formula has been so successful that it has been repeated in duplicate at Disneyworld, Florida. There are also a great many much less ambitious park and zoo pleasure railways in North America, some with steam power but most are driven by internal-combustion.

At one time there were many railroads which

Above : East Broad Top
Railroad's three-foot
gauge 2-8-2 No 12 *Millie*
drops her fire before
going on the turntable
and into the roundhouse
for the night, Rockhill
Furnace, Pennsylvania.
Left : *Millie* (see caption
above) is joined by her
sister locomotive, No 15,
at system headquarters,
Orbisonia, Pennsylvania.
Bottom left : California
Western Railroad's *Skunk*
express on its way
through the redwoods
from Fort Bragg to
Willits; on weekends in
the summer the steam
Super Skunk takes over
Below : This Silverton
Northern Railroad car
has been restored to be
enjoyed by the public.

were built for pleasure in the sense that they took
people to see the scenery or reach the top of a
mountain. Few survived the Model T, but, possibly
because the climb up Mount Washington was a little
too much even for one of Henry Ford's creations, the
most celebrated of them did survive. The eight
remarkable locomotives which make the ascent up
grades as steep as 37 percent have been described in
another chapter. This, the earliest rack-and-pinion
railway in the world, opens for custom daily each
summer.

Most sensible are railways which, while basically
pleasure lines, have some steady income from carrying freight in-between times. For example, the Green
Mountain Railroad at Bellows Falls, Vermont uses
some ex-Canadian Pacific light 4-6-2s to operate its
tourist trains, but Rutland Railroad freights share
the same metals. A further back-up to the system
exists in the huge railroad museum called Steam-
town, creation of clam-shell millionaire and biblical

crusader Nelson Blount, who bought full-size steam locomotives the way ordinary people might collect postage stamps.

The reverse of this arrangement is more common, that is, a freight line which makes a few extra bucks by hauling tourists on a steam train at week-ends. 'Ride the Supper Chief' says the Sierra Railroad of Jamestown, California, familiar to us all from the countless Western movies made there. This refers to its evening dine-out excursions over the 40 miles to Oakdale and back; more normal is the daytime Cannonball, nine miles out and back.

All these operations are essentially railroad by-ways. Speeds over 25 mph are exceptional, as are runs over ten miles in length. Even an ambitious and superb project like the 67-mile Cumbres and Toltee

Scenic RR between Chama and Antonito on the borders of Colorado and New Mexico makes up for its length with an average speed of only 10 mph, too slow, in fact, to go there and back in one day, so passengers return by bus in a mere two hours.

However, the true old-fashioned railroad was not like this; it used big steam power and heavy trains and ran them fast. A very select few of the railroads of North America still keep, basically for publicity reasons, a few noble steamers in working order for special trains. In the USA, Union Pacific and the Southern Railway are the main examples, with Canadian National doing the honors in Canada. The problem is that these locomotives, being so big and powerful, are extremely expensive to maintain and run; before taking out UP's famous 4-8-4 No 8444, for instance, it is necessary to put 25 *tons* of fuel oil in its

tender. SR and CN use locomotives that are a little smaller, but still big enough.

A very few outside organizations manage to own big steam – which is easy – and keep it running – which is not. High Iron Incorporated has a 2-8-4 from the Nickel Plate Road whose inaugural tour crossed the country from the east to be at the golden spike centennial celebrations at Promontory, Utah in 1969. Similarly, the Freedom Train, run in 1975 and 1976 to mark two hundred years of American Independence, had three steam locomotives specially restored to haul it on its moves from city to city. Outstanding among the three was one of Southern Pacific's Daylight 4-8-4s, to which reference has been made. On a side trip during the tour, it hauled a 20-car special from Alexandria to Atlanta, Georgia, weighing 800 tons and touched 79 mph in the process.

In Canada, the government of British Columbia has restored Canadian Pacific's Royal Hudson No 2860. This has been done in CP's own Vancouver shops and the 4-6-4 operates excursions five days a week on the British Columbia Railway from Vancouver to Squamish.

One could hardly omit at least a mention of two other categories, which *de jure* but perhaps not *de facto* belong here. It has already been suggested that with a ten-to-one speed factor in favor of jet aircraft, journeys by train in the 500 miles plus range are made by those who are motivated by the prospect of finding pleasure in the actual journey. If this is true, then Amtrak's and the Canadian long-distance trains must be regarded as trains for pleasure. Lastly, we must not forget the purest form of pleasure trains, the countless legion of miniature and model railways with gauges ranging from 15 inches to $\frac{5}{16}$ of an inch and a variety bewildering in the extreme. Can there be any design of locomotive or car, past or present, which does not exist in model form on some model railroad somewhere?

It is to be hoped that all these great trains will still be with us in 20 years time.

Top left : Cripple Creek & Victor : 0-4-4-0 No 1 *Gold-field* **stands alone at a prairie station.**
Left : West Side & Cherry Valley Railroad's Shay No 8 on trestle at Toulumne, California in the days before the line was altered for tourists.

Top right : The totally restored Rio Grande & Southern 4-6-0 No 20 having finally run out of track.
Above : A popular tourist attraction is the Roaring Camp Depot and its pleasure trains at Felton, California.

TRANSPORTING THE NATIONS' FREIGHT

TRANSPORTING THE NATIONS' FREIGHT

Above : On the central
Vermont section of
Canadian National Rail-
ways, it is Christmas Eve,
1947, as a fast freight
double-headed by 4-8-2
No 602 and 2-10-4 No 701
pauses at Milton for a
passenger express to pass.
Left : A long diesel-
hauled freight of the
Denver & Rio Grande
Western Railroad in the
Ruby Canyon of the
Colorado River.
Preceding spread : An
8500 hp Union Pacific gas-
turbine locomotive hauls
an apparently endless
manifest freight at Dale,
Wyoming.

The final chapter of this book concerns, fittingly, what might fairly be called The Greatest Show on Earth. Although the railroads' now must share the nation's traffic with other forms of transportation, the total number of paying customers is still enormous. It is three times greater, in fact, on a ton-mile basis, than it was in 1910, when horses and mules powered the competition. That it can be, should be and will be better does not prevent one admiring what rail freight movement is today. More than 850 billion ton-miles per year is a lot of railroading; on a typical day some 100,000 loaded cars will set out on an average 500 mile journey.

These figures are large enough to be almost meaningless to many people. In terms of rolling trains one might look at the busiest main line of the USA's most prosperous railroad; that is, Southern Railway's 340 miles of mixed single and double track between Cincinatti and Chattanooga. There might be en route at one moment 25 trains conveying 1800 cars. Loads would vary from a 100-car 'unitrain' weighing 13,000 tons with seven diesel locomotives, three cut in at the center under radio control, to the odd local with 20 or so cars and a single unit loco-motive. Typical would be a train like the so-called 'Sparkplug' (because it conveys auto parts) with perhaps 80 cars and three units and would take about 14 hours to cover the distance, inclusive of stops, and the negotiation of the Cumberland Mountains near the Tennessee-Kentucky State line.

To the watcher the feature of most of the other freights, apart from the locomotives, would be the kaleidoscope of colors and famous names on the cars as each immense train grinds by. Not as spectacular, perhaps, as the Cajon pass in California, used by three transcontinental railroads (UP, SP and Santa Fe), where 65 big freights a day would pass, but still well worth seeing.

Southern's Chattanooga Choo-Choo line is good strong mixed main line railroading; multiply it by two hundred and you get freight movement in North America. Not all railroads are mixed in this way. For example, the purposefully made iron-ore hauler like the Quebec, North Shore and Labrador, built in 1952, exists to haul the mineral wealth from diggings in eastern Labrador, 300 miles to Sept Iles on the St Lawrence River. Loaded ore cars are made up into trains of 14,000 tons weight, which are then rolled over fairly level territory to tide-water at a nice steady 35 mph, using a group of six standard diesels plugged in together. This makes for an easy operation. First, one customer loads his freight, a train-load at a time, at one end of the line and asks that it be carried to the other end. Second, the optimum speed of a stand-alone freight operation is quite low; higher speeds would allow better utilization, but increased maintenance (as well as greater derailment hazard) would swallow the profits. QNS & L is a common carrier, but two weekly trains suffice for

business other than loaded ore cars one way and empty ones the other. Incidentally, passenger service including meals is also offered on them, although they are, of course, primarily for general freight.

Huge trains such as those of the QNS & L make for very economical runs but they represent only one end and very much the best end, of the spectrum of North American railroading. Slotting such immense drags into normal railroad operation poses problems; one line that has faced them is Canadian Pacific, who slot 10,000-ton coal trains from mines inland through the Rockies down to the Pacific Ocean at Vancouver, into their transcontinental varnish and hot-shot freights. Fairly heroic measures are needed; 11 diesel locomotives per train, including slave units cut in at points down the train are provided on certain sectors of the route. Alas, a very small proportion of the continent's traffic is formed in bulk flows of this nature.

At the other extreme is found the independent short line covering a few miles of rusty weed-grown track. Operation is very homespun – there are no work-rules here; the superintendent often doubles as engineer, conductor, track man, vice-president for marketing and so on. Often a small profit is made; in other cases the community which the line serves has to put its communal hand into its communal pocket. But, either way, this sort of operation is useful and appreciated; if it is not, the railroad quietly dies.

Many branch lines, particularly in industrial areas, are, however, owned by the big railroad corporations. It is often difficult for them to operate to advantage, as they are often a long way away. No homespun operation is possible and often a full crew is supplied even if there is only one car and, in consequence, big losses. An excellent trend has begun, by which these sort of branches are, one way and another, going independent but, by and large, branch lines are millstones round the necks of companies who have too many of them.

Customers typically consign a dozen or so cars every day in ten different directions. Thus a railroad has to face the horrendously expensive process of collecting, sorting and marshaling cars in order to accumulate enough to send out worthwhile long-distance trains. At the other end the same costly sequence has to be gone through in reverse before cars finally arrive at their destination. A great deal can be done by improving the sorting yards, but the local freight train which trickles around collecting and delivering cars has so far defied the efforts of the improvers. Often such trains receive a cynical reverse compliment with a name like 'Cannonball'. Railroads with too high a proportion of such Cannonballs often go bankrupt.

One solution is to pass the problem onto the competition, by carrying freight 'piggyback' in road

Top left : A 2-6-6-6 of the Chesapeake & Ohio Railroad steams along the 60-mile climb to Clifton Forge in West Virginia. The coal hoppers are empty on this occasion but if full it would mean that the locomotive would be pulling 8000 tons of coal.
Bottom left : Great Northern's 3600 hp SD-45 diesel locomotive pulls a train with a group of new hi-cube boxcars.
Below : One way of transporting motor vehicles in bulk : A solid train of automobiles moves along the Fraser River in British Columbia.

trailers (or in standard containers) loaded on flatcars and leaving the collection and delivery to road vehicles. Even the degree of accumulation that occurs in this instance is insufficient to make economic the running of full trains of this traffic, but there is usually enough to make it possible to put them into blocks of a dozen or so. These can then be added to a train formed of blocks of other traffic to make an economic load, but each stage of accumulation makes for further delay.

One thing to be thankful for is that the freight train is still a problem – its hybrid cousin the mixed train is not one any longer for the simple reason that it has virtually vanished. The most famous of all American railroad writers, the late Lucius Beebe, wrote lovingly of it in the most famous of all his books, *Mixed Train Daily*, first published in 1947, but reprinted many times since.

It ran on tracks far removed from main lines or main highways and provided total transport for the communities it served. All commodities were carried and, towards the rear, just in front of the caboose, would be a creaky wooden combine coach for passengers. The mixed train was not the most rapid form of transport the world has known: time had to be allowed at stations for taking off and picking up freight cars and, moreover, the light rails, which – traditionally rather than actually – depended on the strong green turf keeping them to gauge, limited the speed. But while it lasted it was a great institution, supporting a quiet and satisfying way of life, without which America is now the poorer.

Even if the 'mixed' has gone, the most important thing in railroading remains as it was. Lucius Beebe recalled (in the first volume of the magazine *Trains*) hearing old President Williamson of the New York Central say, as the Century overtook a hot-shot freight near Elkhart, Indiana . . . 'Look at those high cars roll: finest sight in all the world.'

Right : Southern Pacific's oil-fired cab-in-front Mallet 2-8-8-4 pulls a freight train in front of Mount Shasta, California. Below : Union Pacific's Big Boy 4-8-8-4 No 4018 pulls a freight train. The leading block of cars are reefers which are used to carry fruit grown in California to the cities of the East.

**APPENDIX**

The NMRA (National Model Railroad Association) produces many data sheets outlining railway practices, types of railcars, capacities, codes and so on. Reproduced here in their entirety are the data sheets (D9d and D9e) on train, hand, whistle and fixed signals which follow the general prototype practice as specified for example on the A.A.R. Standard Code Sheets. Of course, individual railroading practices can vary considerably. The information below is compiled by Pierce and Buyse for NMRA and is dated 1950.

AUTOMATIC BLOCK SIGNALS

There are six basic types of operating units used in these signals, each of which can exhibit any of the three basic aspects shown below. One or more operating unit may be used on the same mast.

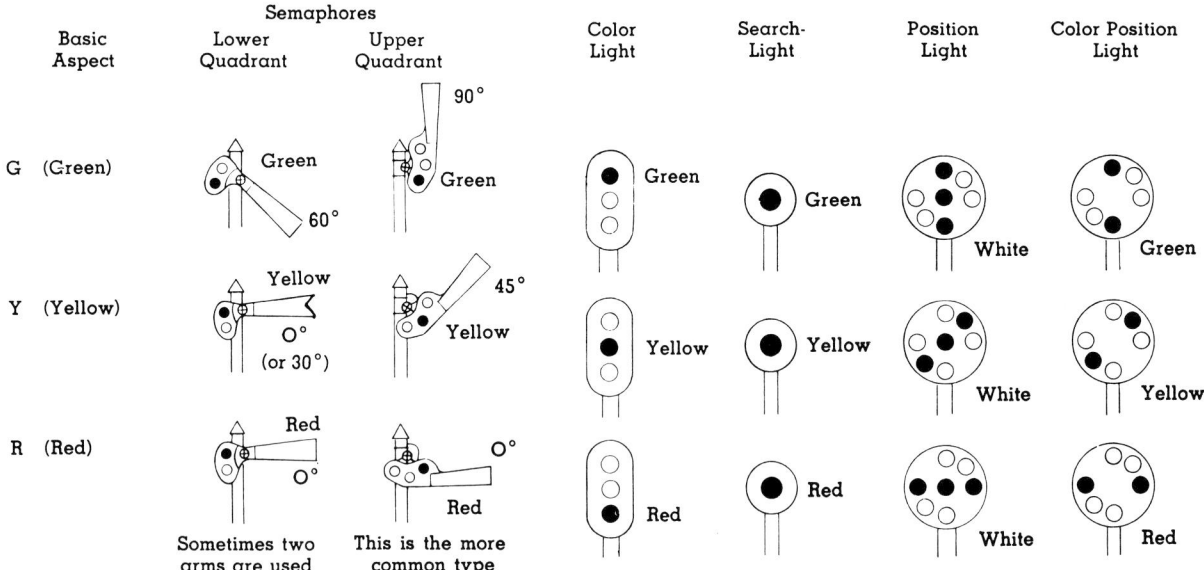

SEMAPHORE SIGNAL BLADES

Pointed End—on permissive automatic block signals.
Square End—on home signals (interlocking, absolute blocks).
Round End—on manual block or train order signals only.
Fish Tail End—on distant or caution signals in lower quadrant system.

NOTE—Most automatic block signals have a marker light or a second operative unit mounted on opposite side of pole below the main operating unit.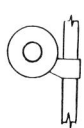

MARKER LIGHTS

A fixed light of either red or lunar white to designate a particular type of signal. They are sometimes used as take siding signals when lighted.

DWARF SIGNALS

These signals may have one or two operating units, either semaphore, searchlight, or position light type. Some railroads use purple in place of red on dwarf signals.

TRAIN ORDER SIGNALS

These signals are located at train order points, i.e., stations and interlocking towers, to notify the train crew to pick up a train order. They are generally manually operated semaphores. They are installed in pairs, one for each direction on opposite sides of the same mast. In manual block territory, the manual block signals serve as train order signals.

INTERLOCKING SIGNALS

These signals consist of two or more operative units of one of the above six basic types mounted one above the other and facing in the same direction to give Absolute Indications. At a junction where two routes diverge, the interlocking signal will often have three operating units, the upper unit giving indications for the straight or high speed route, the middle unit giving indications for the diverging route, and the lower unit covering special routes or movements. For example, the lower unit when in yellow aspect may be a "Call on" signal permitting slow speed operation over a special route such as for switching moves. e.g. See rule 290 on sheet D9e.1.

MISCELLANEOUS FIXED SIGNALS

TRAIN SIGNALS

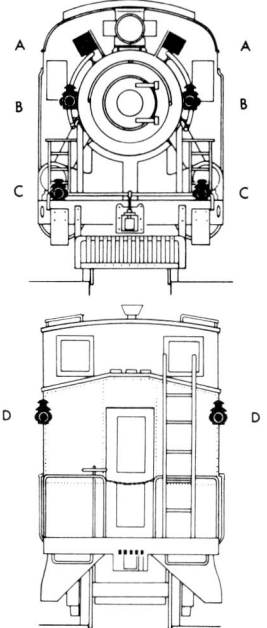

Green flags at AA indicate another section is following. At night green lamps are also displayed at BB.

White flags at AA indicate an extra train. At night, white lamps are also displayed at BB.

If at night and running forward, headlight is lighted. If at night and running backward without cars or at front of train pulling cars, lighted white lamp is displayed at top center of tender.

Marker lamps showing yellow (or green) to the sides and in the direction of motion and red to the rear, lighted at night and unlighted by day, are used as follows:

At CC to indicate engine running backwards without cars or at the rear of a train pushing cars. As an alternate by day, yellow (or green) flags may be displayed at CC.

At DD on caboose or other last car to indicate train running forward. If locomotive is without cars, or at rear of train pushing cars, the lamps are displayed at DD on the tender; if by day, yellow flags may be used instead.

Note 1: Signals at CC may be combined with those at AA and BB to give the corresponding combined indications.

Note 2: Lamps at DD on train clear of main track are turned to show yellow (or green) to rear, sides, and front.

MANUAL SIGNALS

These signals are given with hand, flag, or lamp.

  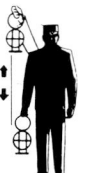    

STOP	REDUCE SPEED	PROCEED	BACK	APPLY BRAKES	RELEASE BRAKES	TRAIN HAS PARTED
Swung across the track.	Held horizontally at arm's length when train is running.	Up and down motion.	Small vertical circle across the track. (M)	Swung above head horizontally when train is running.	Held above head when train is standing.	Large vertical circle across the track when train is running. (N)

ENGINE WHISTLE SIGNALS

• = Short sound (1½ to 2 seconds). ▬ = long sound (2½ to 3 seconds). ▬▬ = extra long sound (5 seconds). Sounds should be distinct with 1 second pause between. A series of short sounds is an alarm for persons or livestock on track.

•	Apply brakes, stop.
▬ ▬	Release brakes, proceed.
▬ • • •	Flagman protect rear of train.
▬ ▬ ▬ ▬	Flagman return from West or South.
▬ ▬ ▬ ▬ ▬	Flagman return from East or North.
▬ ▬ ▬	Train has parted. Repeated until answered by N above. Also used as reply to N.
• •	Answer to signal not otherwise covered.
• • •	When standing, answer to M above or to X below. When running, answer to Y below.
• • • •	Call for signals.

▬ • •	Used to call attention to signals displayed to indicate section following (except to superior trains or those moving in the opposite direction on another track).
▬ ▬ • ▬	Used when approaching public crossings at grade, at curves, and other obscure places; prolong last sound until clear.
▬ ▬ • •	Used as alternate for above signal.
▬	Approaching stations, junctions, tunnels, etc.
• • ▬	Second engineman assume control of brakes.
• ▬	Inspect train line for leak or sticking brakes.
▬ ▬ •	Used as reply to Z below.

COMMUNICATING SIGNALS

Used only by train crews to communicate with engine crews (generally by pulling air signal cords).

• •	When standing—Start.	When running—Stop at once.
• • •	When standing—Back the train. (X)	When running—Stop at next passenger station. (Y)
• • • •	When standing—Apply or release air brakes.	When running—Reduce speed.
• • • • •	When standing—Recall the flagman.	When running—Increase speed.
▬ ▬ • •	Conductor calling engineman's attention to meeting point. (Z)	
• • • • • •	When running—Increase train heat.	
▬ •	When running—Shut off train heat. • ▬ • is also used.	
▬	When running—Brakes sticking, look for hand signals.	

Picture Credits

The Illustrated London News: 11, 8–9, 16, 43 (bottom), 47, 81 (center), 126–127
E J Gulash Collection: 14 (center), 70–71, 74–75, 97 (inset), 100–101, 109 (large), 160 (bottom), 166 (center)
C E Mulvihill: 118–119 (top center)
J M Jarvis Collection: 17 (bottom), 19, 20–21, 31, 36–37, 40, 44–45, 60 (center left), 68 (bottom), 69 (top), 72 (top), 77 (top), 78 (bottom), 78–79, 83 (center), 85 (top), 88 (bottom), 89 (top), 97 (large), 118 (top left), 128, 130 (bottom), 136–137, 142 (top)
V Goldberg Collection: 12, 18, 24, 58 (top), 59 (both), 62 (top left), 63 (top right), 68 (top), 82 (bottom), 83 (bottom), 87 (bottom), 147 (bottom), 171 (top & bottom), 177 (center)
Real Photographs Company: 51 (top right), 56, 61 (top), 62 (left center), 73 (center), 96 (top)
Orbis Publishing Limited: 27 (top)
Rail Photo Service: 28–29
G F Allen Collection: 13, 22–23, 25, 35 (center & bottom), 49 (top), 50, 51 (bottom), 60 (bottom), 61 (bottom 2), 62–63 (top), 64–65, 69 (center), 73 (bottom), 76 (all 3), 77 (bottom), 82–83 (top), 94, 96 (bottom), 99 (bottom right), 103 (top), 106 (bottom), 107 (center right), 112, 114 (bottom left), 115 (top right), 119 (both), 120–121 (all 5 but top right), 123 (top), 124, 129 (both), 130 (center), 131 (both), 134–135 (all 5), 138 (top), 139 (top), 143, 144–145, 148 (bottom), 149 (bottom), 151 (center), 152–153, 154, 155 (bottom), 156 (bottom left), 158 (top & centre left), 159 (top & bottom), 180, 181, 182 (both), 184 (bottom)
P J Howard: 30, 36 (inset), 41, 51 (top left), 53 (top), 121 (top right), 123 (bottom), 138–139 (bottom), 160 (top), 170 (bottom), 172–173 (both)
Amtrak: 102 (top), 157 (bottom), 158 (bottom)
T B Keer: 118 (bottom)
M Befeler: 86 (center), 114–115 (bottom)
Santa Fe RR: 124
Canadian Pacific Railway: 42, 43 (top), 45 (inset), 46. 50 (top), 105 (inset), 108 (center), 117 (all 3), 122 (bottom), 125 (bottom), 139 (bottom right), 156–157 (top), 183
Canadian National Railway: 44 (inset), 50 (center), 51 (bottom right), 125 (top)
Union Pacific Railroad: 108 (bottom), 146
J Shaughnessy: 49 (bottom), 52, 80 (top), 89 (bottom & center), 149 (top)
Southern Pacific RR: 90 (top left), 150 (top)
Cutler Collection: B F Cutler 69 (bottom), 90–91 (top center), 151 (bottom), 171 (center)
B F Culter 69 (bottom), 90–91 (top center), 151 (bottom), 171 (center)
R L Lorenz: 174–175 (top)
Paul S Stephanus: 175 (top left)
G M Best: 88 (top)
J B Snell: 168–169
J A Rehor: 86 (bottom)
D Duke: 176 (bottom)
E Lambert: 79 (center)
P Huntingdon: 79 (bottom), 164–165
H W Pontin: 91 (top right)
J T Shackleton Collection: 32 (top), 34, 35 (top), 103 (bottom), 107 (bottom left & right), 110–111, 122 (top), 143 (bottom), 148 (center), 154, 178–179, 185